Omadhaun Acres

Growing up Irish in Emerald Wisconsin

by

Larry Moore

Table of Contents

Dedication

Note from the Author

Glossary, Definitions and Odd Explanations

Main Characters

Chapter 1....Winter was cold

Chapter 2....Rocks of Ages

Chapter 3....The Holy Trinity of Farming

Chapter 4....Answering the 'Call'

Chapter 5....Fork on the Right

Chapter 6...."Mary, can you lighten the picture a little?"

Chapter 7....Potato Vines (The Irish version of <u>Roots</u>)

Chapter 8....The Power and the Glory

Chapter 9....Where is Barry Fitzgerald When You Really Need Him?

Epilogue

Dedication

To my beloved sons Jeff and Mike; everything I know about love came from Emerald and your Mother. From the moment you were born I promised to give you all that I was. I hope I gave as much love as I feel I got back.

In Memory of

Mom, Dad, Irv and all in this story ... I wish I could tell you just how extraordinary ordinary was. Thank you.

Note from the Author

This is one man's attempt at telling parts of his life story with varying parts of historical accuracy, 'literary license', and the Moore style of love and humor.

I did not research this book, and I did not intend for it to be a text on rural life. I wrote the story of one extended family from my personal recollections, and I wrote it the way I remembered it. .. or want to remember it! If you want to read a real book written by a real author may I recommend Noel Perrin's "First Person Rural".

God Bless my beloved wife Mania who took on the task of editing my writing, because I write like the Moore's sing. We may be the only ones who enjoy it.

My maternal Irish Grandma once told her son, "Thomas, you could spend half an hour talking to the barn door."

Mania will get her own pass key from St. Peter for just living with me, and gets all the credit for any semblance of structure in this book.

Glossary, Definitions and Odd Explanations

The title comes from one of Dad's favorite sayings "He's an omadhaun ape". I was finally able to find a definition of omadhaun in one of those huge dictionaries in the library. The one that would give you a hernia if you tried to pick it up. The definition of omadhaun (pronounced 'ah ma don') is… "(Irish) a foolish man or boy (from Irish Gaelic *amadán*]'. So it comes from the Auld Sod and was a word passed down from his ancestors, and the 'ape' was just one of my Dad's flourishes.

Names used in this book are mostly true, because they were good and true friends and neighbors of my family. Please take no offense as they are used with love and happy memories and the laughter that was so much a part of my growing up.

The vernacular in the book is the common language used on the farm. So 'shit' means manure and isn't a swear word, "Saints preserve us".

The locale is Emerald Township, in Western Wisconsin. It's about 50 miles west of Minneapolis and St. Paul MN and the location of our family farm. Emerald Township is next to Erin township, the location of St. Patrick's (Catholic Church, heavily attended by the Irish in the area] and Erin Corners. Erin Corners, or simply Erin is the name for the junction of County Rd T and County Rd G, which was the original location of Red Higgins' store, a combination bar, barber, and grocery establishment.

Mow. It's a noun and a verb and they were used commonly in my family. They are pronounced differently.

> You mow (rhymes with no] the hay and…
> put it in the hay mow (rhymes with cow).

Main Characters

☐ Author: Larry Moore (Lawrence D. Moore) Larry was born in 1946.

☐ Dad: Lawrence E. Moore

☐ Mom: Mary Elizabeth (Dean) Moore or referred to as Mary Dean to keep her separated from all the other Marys in the family.

☐ Irv: Dad's brother, born Henry Irvin Moore. His wife was Mary Murtha Moore, referred to as Mary Irv.

☐ Margie: My sister Margaret (Moore)Yakos. Her nickname came from me because I couldn't pronounce Margaret. It is pronounced mah-gee with a (g) as in good, not a (g) as in giant, and no (r) sound.

☐ Mania: My wife Mania (Kizen) Moore, her first name is pronounced mahn-ya

Chapter 1

Winter Was Cold

Now there is a profound statement! No wonder you are reading my work with a sense of awe and wonder. Shakespeare and Hemingway take a back seat and learn from the master!

Actually winter in Emerald Wisconsin WAS cold. But like so many other events in my life, we did not know we were cold in winter. We were just having winter. When I went to college, one of my English classes had a unit on great Russian authors. One of the short stories we were assigned was Gogol's "The Overcoat."

Now these dudes were cold.

I do not know if the temperature in Russia is significantly colder that what we experienced in Emerald. What I do know is that unlike Gogol's characters we were physically cold but not cold in hope and spirit. My experiences did not leave me hopeless and hollow and depressed nor angry and bitter at my world. Quite to the contrary, my experiences were cold and often painful, yet in an almost contradictory way they were filled with challenge and pride and dare I say almost fun.

I look back on Emerald winters with so many wonderful memories and impressions that while not wanting to experience them ever again; I know I am the person I am now because of those experiences.

The official beginning of winter was not on the calendar but with your underwear. When it got cold enough for the 'long johns', it was winter. I think one could study the anthropology of our society by the evolution of underwear. Early Emerald denizens wore long woolen underwear 365 days a year. They argued that these 'union suits' kept you warm in winter and actually kept you cooler in the summer by absorbing the sweat.

Ah yes! Long woolen garment, summer temperatures, intense labor in the fields, and maybe a once-a-week bath! The Wisconsin pun of 'Come Smell Our Dairy Air' takes on so many odiferous meanings and spellings!

In my youth I was lucky enough that I did not have to deal with wool but rather nice comfortable cotton long johns. One quickly learned the horror of the 'one piece death trap'. Never and I repeat never put on the one piece outfit over the top of the summer briefs! Sensitivity to the faint of heart prevents me from detailing that first stroke of panic and the ensuing wrestling match as I tried to 'heed the call of nature' in the outhouse while wearing both briefs and 'trap-door long johns'.

I don't remember any of the Russian characters having to take their shoes off so they could take their pants off so they could take their underwear off so they could take their briefs down. Tragedy? Comedy? This may be the origin of the word tragic-comedy!

As a child I loved stories, fables and tales. One of my favorite was about the ant and the grasshopper. While the frivolous grasshopper whiled away the time being lazy and playing his fiddle, the energetic ant increased his already hectic life getting ready for winter. The message of the fable was that as the grasshopper suffered and froze, the prudent and hard working ant was safe and warm in his lair.

Like the ant, as winter approached our pace seemed to increase with a slightly thrilling anticipation of impending winter. The days would shorten, the cool weather replaced summer's heat, and with most of the harvest safely in the barn and granary we now turned to 'winterizing' the farm.

Loose hay filled the mow (remember, rhymes with cow) to a depth of over thirty feet. This would be fed to the animals through the winter months, but it also offered great insulation. Calves and heifers would be brought in from the summer pasture which would increase body heat in the barn. The milk cows and horses would be in the barn most of the time, also adding to the heat factor.

Canvas and secondary doors would cover the existing doors to stop the wind and keep in as much heat as possible. When it was extra windy and below zero we would pack a mixture of straw and manure at the base of the doors to stop drafts. In the morning this would be frozen like cement, and would have to be chipped out before the doors could open.

And why would we open the doors? Because... every single morning the manure had to be scooped out of the gutters, and thrown into a manure bucket. Now this was a work of engineering art that even the pharaohs could appreciate. Running the width of the barn plus an extra 20 feet outside was an I-beam track. This track was suspended by hooks and screws inside the barn, and then to a 20 foot horizontal pole outside. The horizontal pole was then supported by a 20 foot tall vertical pole. The I-beam track supported a carriage that was connected to a half-barrel that was locked into an 'open end up' position. We would use forks and shovels to fill the barrel with manure, and then push the whole 'trolley system' outside where it would be suspended over the horse drawn manure spreader. A lever would be pulled, and the whole contraption would spin sideways depositing its contents into the spreader. About 10 repeats would empty the gutters.

The really fun part was if the temperature and wind were miserable; we would keep the doors shut until the bucket was full. Then Dad would open the barn door, and as rapidly as possible he would insert the 4 foot removable section of track that allowed the door to be shut. He would have to raise the I-beam and hook it. Then two sliding couplers would complete the track. On a signal either my uncle or I would push the manure bucket through the door, dump it as fast as possible, and return inside. Then Dad would disassemble the track and close the door to keep the cold out and the heat inside.

It was important to keep the barn warm, partly for the health of the animals, but mainly to keep the water system from freezing. Like Noah on the Ark, our animals two-by-two shared a watering cup. If they pressed the suspended paddle in the cup with their nose, water squirted into the cup so they could drink. However, all the cups and pipes were exposed to the air so if the barn temperature dropped below freezing, the cups and pipes would freeze. At best the animals would be thirsty, and a thirsty cow does not produce as much milk. At worst the pipes could freeze so hard the expanding pipes would rupture under the ice pressure.

I remember one time Dad, Irv, and I with our bare hands wrapped around a water pipe trying to warm it enough to break an ice block. We would take turns breathing on the pipe also, until

Dad decided that his brother's love of onions and horse radish made his breath so bad he was willing to let the SOB pipe freeze! Then the three of us would stand there and laugh at each other. I am not sure if old Nikkoli Gogol would have found humor in this moment. Maybe it is just all too Irish.

OK, back to the manure. The spreader would now be full. Delicate men in romantic times called the cargo 'night soil'. Learned scientific men referred to the contents as fertilizer. Biologists would call it manure or fecal matter. We called it shit.

The spreader was a rectangular box on wheels that had a double set of rotating beaters at the back end. When a lever was engaged the beaters would rotate while a revolving track system would pull the cargo into the beaters. The faster the horses pulled, the faster the system worked, and the farther the cargo would be spread on the land. A good team of horses, well driven, could empty that cargo over a wide area in no time. I have never had trouble understanding the expression, "When the shit hits the fan!"

When I was first old enough to be trusted with a team in the field, one of my first and most lasting lessons was ALWAYS check the wind. I learned quickly but sadly the dangers of unloading with the wind to your back, because it was more than wind that was hitting your back!

I remember coming back to the barn with some very organic decorations on my cap and jacket. There stood Dad and Irv with big silly grins on their faces, and they both licked their fingers and put them in the air, saying, "Isn't the wind from the south today?"

Of course if the temperature and snow made it impossible to use the spreader we often fell back on option number two. The Sleigh!

The U.S. Postal Service had the motto: "Neither snow nor rain nor gloom of night stays these couriers from the swift completion of their appointed rounds." Dad had a similar motto: "The shit must get spread." Although we weren't spreading mail, IT had to get out and be delivered every morning! If the spreader wouldn't work, out came the sleigh.

The sleigh was a set of two skis connected to another set of two skis by cross-chains. This formed a 4-foot wide 'double bunk' system that was covered by twelve 2 x 4 rough cut planks that were bracketed at 4 points, one each at the outside edge of the double bunks.

Picture this. The sleigh is parked under the manure track. Then the cargo is loaded. The snow is deep and the temperature is sub-zero. We head into the field to deposit our 'organic fertilizer'. We were 'green' well before it became politically correct. We were green....except for our fingers, toes, ears, and face. They were red or white....as in frost bite.

More than once the story repeats. Dad, Irv and me on the sleigh.....oh hell, it is a friggin' sled! A manure sled! Sleighs are what Bing Crosby's girl friend rode in "Holiday Inn" or what people road over the river and through the woods to grandma's house.

We had a shit sled.

The horses are straining to pull the load through the ice crushed snow. Pink, bloody tracks show up where their legs got slashed by the icy crust. It is so cold and the leather lines to the horses are so stiff it is like reining with cane poles. Our hands are so cold that we must wear leather 'chopper' mitts lined with home-knitted wool liners. Even then the fork handles feel like icicles and the cargo is starting to freeze. Dad and Irv's glasses are frosted over, and the horses have icicles dangling from their nose hairs.

As the cargo is slowly off-loaded a new problem develops. Without the weight of the cargo, each individual 2 x 4 plank looses the ability to balance all of us. As the load disappears, we start playing 'foot piano' with the boards. If there isn't a corresponding weight at one end, the other end will just flip. I remember stepping on one plank that had no one on the other end. Down I went, plank up, me flat on my back in the snow. And there are Dad and Irv leaning on their forks, grinning like moronic idiots, and Dad says, "Are you going to make a snow angel?"

Gogol would not have understood the pithy humor of this moment!

Manure off-loaded.
Sled planks cleaned, turned and cleaned again.

Back to the barn, and the horses cuts are cleaned and treated with iodine.

Now we must care for the 'young stock' which consisted of the calves, heifers, and a few young bulls. They had to be watered because they did not have water cups in their pens. They had to be let out of the barn and watered in a big tank next to the well and milk house. The 'horse tank' was a 4 foot by 20 foot metal tank that was filled directly from the well. Water would run from the well pump down a pipe into a holding tank that cooled the milk cans. The excess water from the cooling tank would run by pipe through the wall of the milk house into the horse tank. In the summer this huge tank would water all of our animals.

When it got cold we would have to 'winterize' the tank. That meant covering the whole tank with boards. The last five boards would be nailed together, and have a hinge. Then the whole tank would be covered with our famous straw and manure concoction, up to several feet thick. This would keep the water in the tank from freezing.

Twice a day we would uncover the west end of the tank, and using the five hinged boards we would open the tank. Then the 'young stock' would be let out of the barn, and they would sprint to the tank to get their water. When the last had drunk its fill, they would be herded to the barn, and the five-hinged boards would be closed, and the manure insulation would be re-piled on the tank.

Now that the cattle and horses were cared for, it was time to care for the chickens. Water was hauled to the chickens in 5 gallon pails. (Each pail weighed about 40 pounds.) Two 5 gallons pails of water can be fun in the warmth of summer. Just think of the fun of hauling two 5 gallons pails of water across a snow filled barnyard in sub zero weather.

We could use an Olympic grading system to determine the skill and performance in completing this task. To arrive at the chicken house with two full pails was a perfect 10. I was more likely to achieve a lower score. Being short was no advantage. Wanting to fill the water tanks with only one trip meant filling the pails to the top, which almost guaranteed point deductions for spillage. Spillage not only led to deductions, more importantly it lead to wet pants. Wet pants lead immediately to frozen stiff pants in winter.

The advantage of caring for the chickens was in the area of sinus health. For the rest of my life I have not come across an over-the-counter treatment for breathing irregularities to rival chicken shit, ah, excrement. Country boy attempts to be sophisticated. As you would walk into a chicken coop 3 out of 5 of your senses experience Armageddon. Nasal hairs are seared, sinuses deep in your head explode out of anger, and a mid-west level Height-Asbury buzz hits your senses. Your eyes water and burn; you can taste chicken…chicken feathers, chicken breath, and chicken shit.

Colonel Sanders, I want to kill you!

The water was dumped into long shallow watering troughs which were covered with thin wire grates that had openings wide enough for the chickens to get their heads inside and drink. The covering grates were to allow the chickens room for drinking but prevent them from getting inside the trough. You see chickens will walk in anything. They will walk in their water containers, they will walk in their food containers, and it is impossible for a chicken to walk very far without dropping a little gift from their feathered colon. Given a chance they will despoil their drinking water and their food source.

I can still see the special little shovel that hung on the wall of the chicken coop. The shovel was just the size of the inside of the drinking trough, and there were holes in the shovel to let the water pass through. So every morning the grate cover would be flipped open, and the little shovel put in one end of the trough, and you would walk the whole length of the trough, skimming out any poop that managed to fall through the grate.

Next came the oyster shells. Everyone knows birds do not have teeth. They also don't have lips or an opposable thumb, but that is not part of this story. Birds must find sand, rocks, gravel or general 'grit' to swallow. Some of this is retained in a special organ called the gizzard or 'crop'. Food such as oats, corn or other grains are swallowed whole and then pass into the crop where the grit serves as a grinding agent, breaking down seeds so the bird can digest the food.

The chickens were locked inside most of the time, partly because of the winter weather but also it was easier to collect their eggs if the birds were in a confined area. By being locked in, the birds were denied access to natural sources of grit, so we would offer them a simple gravity-fed feeder full of ground up oyster shells that could be purchased at the local feed mill. The oyster shells also supplemented the chicken's diet, giving minerals that allowed the chicken's body to produce the shell that surrounds and protects the eggs they laid. It was really weird to reach up and into a nesting box, and grab a shell-less egg. These are a totally perfect egg except for the fact there is no shell. The egg is just a gelatinous mass surrounded by a membrane, which feels kind of like a baggie full of warm Jello.

The eggs were Irv's little cottage industry. It didn't matter who picked the eggs, they were delivered to Irv's house. We would keep out enough for breakfast or baking but the rest went to Irv. He would wash them in his special bowl and scrub them with his special brush. Then each egg was 'candled'. Originally a real candle was used, but any light source would work. The egg would be held in front of the light and if you could see a dark little mass inside the egg you knew Mr. Rooster had been courting. The local egg dealer would not buy fertilized eggs because he could not re-sell them for marketing.

If it were getting close to spring, these fertilized eggs would be brought back to a 'nesting hen' for 'brooding'. Usually this old hen would accept these few eggs along with her own eggs. This adoption was often easiest if you could leave the eggs while she was out eating and drinking. Since chickens have very short memories and we never taught ours how to count, the returning hen just squatted on any eggs in her nest. If this adoption method did not work, we sometimes would incubate some eggs in the house. We would wrap the eggs in a towel and place them on or near the heating stove in the living room. Timing was important in this operation because it takes 21 days for an egg to hatch.

Our annual routine dictated that in the first week of March we would drive to Star Prairie where Mr. Utgard had a hatchery, and there we would purchase a box of chicklets. Ha, just a little Irish humor there.

Actually we would purchase 50 little chicks which were put into a 'chick box' which had four sections for safe spacing. Of course this was Advanced Math for the Moore's. How do you divide 50 by 4 and make it equal? The Bible's Old Solomon might have had an answer but we usually settled on the safe and sane 12 and 14, 12 and 12. Easy to count by two's, and no one had to use that number that exists between 12 and 14. Not that traditional rural Irish Catholics were superstitious mind you! Saints be praised!

So the box of chicks would come home, and be placed on the stove. Any of our own brood would then be added to the 'chick box' which would be their home for several days. The box was big enough for 50 chicks to grow for a while. The box was heavy cardboard with vent holes in the side and in the removable top. The top was necessary because while chicks could not fly, they were good little jumpers, and you didn't want flightless little yellow peeps sky diving off the top of the oil burner.

Of course we were concerned about the safety of the chicks, because if you just paid real hard earned cash for these birds you had to guard your investment. Safety was always a factor when you removed the cover, which was necessary to feed them. So it was often a two or three person job to feed and water the chicks. One person would remove the cover, and be the 'jumper-stopper'. The second person would re-fill the chick-meal container, while the third person re-filled the water container. Persons two and three had the added responsibility of poop removal. Remember, chickens walk through their nourishment. It is a rule!

So while persons two and three were doing the dirty work, it was the 'jumper-stopper' who had the stress job. The top of our Jungers oil burner was over 4 feet off the floor, so from that height any little peep that hit the floor was a dead bird. Just as an aside here, if you ever look at cartoons showing a dead bird the cartoonist always puts an X where the eyes were. I hate to say it, but I have seen a lot of dead birds and the do look like that! There eyes close up, and they do look like an X.

To protect the birds and the investment we sometimes put the box on the floor to care for them. OK, can you see this coming? The box had six inch sides, so the jumper-stopper was on his hands and knees trying to keep the birds inside. If the bird made it over the side they only fell six inches, and always survived. Survival leads to a mad dash all around the house in a panic run to freedom. Watch chickens. They never run in a straight line! Can you see it? Can you see a four inch tall ball of yellow down zigzagging across the floor, slipping on the linoleum, tripping on the throw rugs, darting under chairs and tables and sofas? Sofas are the worst because they can actually fit under the damn thing, and you have to tip the sofa to find them, but of course you have to be careful tipping it so you don't crush the chick. At this point the chick dashes off to safety under the oil burner.

Do you need much imagination to see three people bent at the waist, being careful not to step on the chicks, chasing at least one chick......ooops, who the hell left the cover off the box, because now there are more damn chicks making a break for freedom.

I think this is when I first learned to curse!

If we timed the purchase of the chicks with the arrival of spring, the little darlings would soon be transferred out to the 'brooder house'. Have you noticed how we have such clever and exotic names for things? Like the chicken coop had chickens inside; the hay mow was full of hay; the milk house stored milk; and the horse stalls were for horses. Clever lot we Moore's. So I will break it to you slowly. The 'brooder house' was where we put little chicks to be 'brooded' until they lost their down, and became teenagers with real feathers.

Instead of using a real hen to warm the chicks we used a special heating lamp. The lamp was suspended by chains so it could be lowered or raised depending on the size of the birds and the outside temperature. Colder temperatures meant the lamp must be lowered so the birds can bask in more heat. On a cold morning you could look in the window and see one big yellow ball cuddled right under the lamp. You couldn't see feet or eyes or beaks, just a single mass of peep down.

So I have been wandering all over telling my story, and it is that age-old puzzle...what came first, the chicken story or the egg story? You decide.

Another puzzle is that after all these years it just dawned on me. I had mentioned that selling eggs was Irv's little cottage industry. But just where was he during all the work? Did Irv haul water on frigid winter days? Did Irv scoop poop out of their water? I must have missed him that week that we had chicks on the stove or during the 'keystone cops' chick-chase? I do remember hauling the eggs to Irv, but I don't remember sharing in the profits. I guess that is just one of the benefits of being the alpha male in our clan.

Life outside was cold during the winter, but it could also get cold inside. We lived in a big old farm house, which was built long before the concept of insulation was popular. I think the simple truth was they had no good insulation, but they did have lots of fuel and it was cheap. In the basement was a wood burning furnace.

By the time I was born they were burning coal instead of wood, because most of the trees in the area were gone. The original trees were home cut and sawed to build all the houses, barns, and sheds. The remaining trees were corded for heat. Now that coal could be easily and cheaply shipped to Emerald and Cylon most of the farmers switched to heating with coal. The few trees that remained were viewed as 'the enemy' by most farmers because you had to plow around them, which is yet another story best told at a different time.

The furnace was in the basement, and directly above it was a huge metal grate that allowed radiant heat from the furnace to rise from the basement to the rest of the house. The grate was situated roughly in the center of the house, and right at the base of the stairs to the second floor. There was also a one foot by one foot grate in the ceiling of the living room that could be opened to allow heat to rise into the northeast bedroom upstairs. That was our heating system. On extremely cold nights that furnace would be stoked to the maximum, and the grate would be so hot you didn't want to touch the metal, and yet the rest of the house was freezing!

I remember Mom had various sites where she placed Holy Water so we could bless ourselves often. One of the sites was a small jar with a metal lid that sat on the window sill at the top of the stairs, located so we all could bless ourselves every night and then every morning. Well on some winter nights that whole jar of Holy Water was frozen solid. As a child I often wondered why God would let His water freeze, but that theological problem is for someone else to solve.

In an attempt to add more heat to the house Dad purchased a Jungers stove. Technically it was a kerosene burner, but again the Moore's were often short on 'technical'. The Jungers was a two-burner kerosene stove. It had a tank on the back side that would be filled with kerosene or Number Two Oil (whatever that meant!). You would turn a spigot, wait a few minutes, and reach inside with a good old farmers match to light one of the burners. The amount of heat was controlled by the amount of kerosene you let flow through the spigot. If you wanted more heat, allow more oil. If it was really cold you would light the second burner and open the spigot to full. This stove was located on a wall with a chimney that separated the kitchen from the dining room.

I remember coming in from outside and basically undressing by the Jungers. Cold and wet caps, gloves, shoes, and pants or bibs would be arranged in various locations on or under the stove. The long johns were left on, but not out of a sense of modesty. If you really needed to warm up you would rotate between hugging the stove and leaning backwards against it, and that my dear would require some type of clothing for protection. Many times I remember getting warm that way, then taking a pillow for my head and laying on the floor on my back with my feet on the stove. I do remember falling asleep in that position, and often thought I was really no different than the peeps under the heating lamp!

Hands and feet were the worst problem in the cold. Obviously the quality of clothing in modern times exceeds anything we had in 'the good old days'. There were heavy leather 'chopper mitts' with wool liners, but there were simply so many tasks that could not be done while wearing mittens. And those old yellow 'farmer gloves' just didn't supply the warmth that was needed. So between light gloves and bare hands work, by the end of winter our hands would have ugly and sore 'freeze cracks' at the tips and around the nails. There was no avoiding them, and very few creams could cure them.

One of the best was a brand called Cornhusker's which, if you are familiar with it, was like clear snot but it helped a little. The ultimate treatment

was in the barn and was something we did not discover. Someone suggested rubbing our hands with something called 'udder balm' which was a treatment salve for cows damaged udders and teats. We felt kind of foolish at first, but we soon discovered that it worked better than anything. It came in a quart sized jar, the first plastic container I remember, now you can get Udder Balm in a cute little jar decorated with black and white cow spots. But nothing was perfect, and one of my weird yet lasting memories of my Dad was the terrible cracks he would get in his usually incredibly soft hands.

The good old Jungers played a role in bedtime preparation. I would strip down to my long underwear, get as close to the stove as possible. My pillow would be lying on top of the stove, storing as much heat as a feather pillow could hold. Then I'd sprint to my bedroom, jump under four layers of blankets and quilts while holding the warm pillow. I would lie on my side and 'run in place' under the covers trying to use friction to warm the bed plus keep my blood pumping through my body. Finally part of my head and part of the pillow would emerge from under the covers. After that it was all body heat for the night. If the temperature was low enough in the morning the frost on the windows would be so thick you could not see through the glass. More than once I woke up to find a small snow drift on the sill, blown in over night by a strong north wind. Often the electric outlet on my north wall was so coated with frost that it was unusable, and we were probably lucky that this didn't cause some kind of arc which could have started a fire.

If you needed to use the bathroom during the night, the bathroom was just down the hall. The bathroom was actually a 2 gallon metal chamber pot with a matching cover. It just sat there in the corner of the hallway; one pot, no privacy. So if the call of nature hit, you crawled out of your warm bed into a freezing room, scurry down a cold hallway, and gently lower yourself on to an ice cold metal pot. Let's just say there was no cute little stand full of reading material in this bathroom. Speed meant survival.

In the morning the last person to wake up was usually the last person to use the pot. That person then won the bonus award of hauling the whole pot outside and down to the Official Moore Bathroom, also lovingly referred to as 'the old 3-holer', yes, the outhouse. Oh, for the wanton luxury and decadence. A door with an eye-hook guaranteed privacy. Wood instead of metal surrounded your parts. We had a choice of 3 different size holes, with one hole cut half the height of the other two. Hey, if Goldilocks wandered into this cottage just think how that tale would have changed.

Of course my sister and I fought. But when Mom had enough, we did not get a 'time out'. She would simply say, "So which of you wants 'pot duty' for a whole week?" I think this kind of threat could end the Arab-Israeli conflict. I remember later in life listening to some of my 'town friends' tell about how they had forgotten to flush the toilet a couple of times, and how their parents had made them stand by the toilet and keep flushing until they promised to always remember to flush. One said they were so embarrassed that they started to cry. Even now I fail to see the punishment in this, but as a child I was totally bewildered.

OK, let me go through this again.

You get to go into a warm room and use the toilet?

Yes.

You get to simply push a lever and all the waste disappears?

Yes.

You were made to stand there and keep pushing the lever and watching water swirl down the toilet?

Yes.

And this reduced you to tears and taught you a lesson?

Yes.

Hello! This is not a punishment. This is better than any of the rides or games at the St. Croix County Fair! In fact YOU go to the fair, and I will come to your house to suffer the dreaded 'toilet torture'.

Let's just say the bathroom issue was a challenge. But then so was anything dealing with water. Monday was laundry day. Mom would wheel out the wringer-washer machine, and fill it with water heated on the kitchen stove. In would go a load. My sister was older so her tasks were different, and often more complicated. On wash day, Margie would do some baking or mending or even some ironing. I hauled wet clothes. Coveralls, bibs, and jeans were a struggle for me. First they would be washed, and then Mom would run them through the wringer to get out most of the water. Mom and I would bundle ourselves up in the winter, and carry the laundry basket out to the clothes lines. I could not reach the lines at first so I would hold clothes pins and hand her individual items to hang. In the winter, the items would usually freeze before they were fully dry, so Mom and I would head back out later to haul in the wash. A basket was of no use because nothing folded. Socks, towels, shirts weren't too bad, but damn those coveralls. They were not cloth any more; they were sheets of plywood cut in the shape of coveralls. You did not haul in the clothes, you wrestled them in. If you could imagine trying to move a 5 foot tall frozen gingerbread man, in knee deep snow, while being warned to not drop him at the same time, those are some of my lasting memories of laundry day.

And of course school did not close for the winter. It was cold in school but it was cold everywhere, so it was no big deal. I went to a one-room rural school named Oakdale. It was much like home in that it was a big building (by our standards) with no insulation, poor windows and doors, a huge coal burner in the basement, and two outhouses, one for the boys and one for the girls.

Everyone dressed the same, that meaning as warm as possible. All the boys dressed like me, so your 'good school clothes' eventually became you old work clothes. Everyone wore jeans or bibs or even the dreaded coveralls. You were really lucky if you made it a whole school year with some patches, but what stuck with me was that some Mothers either didn't know how to patch, or maybe they just didn't care. Mom's patches were always of matching material (denim on denim, cotton on cotton) and often came very close to matching. And for sure the thread would not clash with the material, and often was a perfect match. She had a drawer full of 'patch equipment' that could meet almost any need.

I remember a blue bag with white flowers and a drawstring top that was about the size of a 5-pound bag of sugar. Only this bag was full of buttons! Just buttons…buttons of every size, shape and description. She had needle after needle for every job possible, and a metal thimble always near by. When an article of clothing was no longer wearable, she would cut pieces out of it and save them for patches. Any possible remnants could be ripped into strips and sold to 'the rug man' who occasionally passed through.

That was one of my first school lessons. It did not matter what you wore, what mattered was if it was clean, and if it was well cared for. The price, the quality, the quantity of clothes made no difference. It was the attitude of the person wearing the clothes that mattered. Even today I cannot break the habit of 'work clothes' and 'good clothes'. It was ingrained in us that the minute you come home, off go the 'good clothes' and on go the 'work clothes'. Can you relate to this? Can you relate to "….and you better be wearing clean underwear in case you go to the hospital…"? How many of you have dealt with emptying your parent's house after they have passed away, and found unopened packages of under garments hidden in drawers being saved for an emergency?

It was at school that I learned that Mom was a good cook. Well actually it was at school and on fall thrashing rounds (harvesting oats) that I learned some people can cook and others either can't or won't. Since all the school kids were the children of neighbors, and it was these same neighbors we thrashed with, the stories can be blended. There was a period at Oakdale when the parents decided at the annual school meeting to supply the students with a hot noon meal. Each week two different families (read two Mothers) would prepare, deliver, and serve a meal. Just like during thrashing times, some days were like Thanksgiving while others were like wilderness survival.

I remember thrashing on some farms and we could find all kinds of breakdowns, problems, or even lame horses so we could drag out the time...and get to eat the meals prepared by the lady of the house. For some of these ladies, I know it was almost a competition to see who could gain bragging rights of being the best cook. We are talking about the full 'farmers meal' of meat and potatoes and gravy, but also desserts. Pies! One pie...two cuts, so each piece is a quarter of a whole pie. And there was no 'or', it wasn't pie or cake, it was pie and cake.

And then there was Alice. Her name was not Alice but "...the names have been changed to protect the guilty..." You hustled when you thrashed at Alice's farm. Hustled? You hurried the horses! It looked like scenes from the old

Oklahoma land rush out in the field. The silent yet understood message was, "Let's get the hell out of here before we have to eat!" But you could never finish a field before lunch. Alice's meals hit the trifecta: they were small, they were undercooked, and they tasted terrible. As a bonus, Alice was not a housekeeper. Snowball is to hell as Alice is to soap! I swear I saw this with my own bulging eyes. Alice came to the table carrying 8 glasses of water…four in each hand, with her fingers stuck way down into the water like she had 4-fingered bowling balls.

No group of cloistered monks ate so quiet and so fast. No grace, no talking, no lingering over dessert and coffee. The old Pony Express made longer stops than we did at Alice's.

So can you imagine a week of Alice preparing meals for school kids? Here I developed a life long rule: food can be hot, food can be cold…. it just can't be both at the same time! Rule number two: food can be soft, food can crunch….you just can't have soft food that crunches! Salad can crunch, fruits can crunch, and nuts can crunch. Mashed potatoes should not crunch. Double it up…. potatoes should not be hot and cold, or soft and crunchy at the same time. I swear this is the period where I developed a highly sensitive gag reflex. Ask my wife, I still don't mix foods, I like nuts, I like brownies, and I don't like nuts in brownies.

Oakdale was a one room school with all eight grades, and when I was there it had a peak attendance of 32 students. Eight grades, 32 students, one teacher. And I grew up wanting to be a teacher! Yes, it was cold and the meals could be a challenge, but that was nothing compared to the memories and impressions of Oakdale. Eight grades, 32 students…so we learned 'cooperative education' before some genius coined the phrase.

I think winter was the real educator at Oakdale. Everyone was poor; everyone was cold, so let's all make the best of it. We helped each other with school work, and we took care of each other during recess. Recess was 32 kids outside, on their own, with no adult supervision. Can you imagine that today? We made our own rules, and they better be fair. We were all poor farm kids, and many of the kids even had to wear their 'work clothes' to school. No one was teased because of the clothes they wore, because no one was really dressed any better.

Let me try this one as an example of a 'leveling experience'. Some of the boys had to work in the barn before school, and then they wore their barn clothes to school. Having worn the same yellow farmer gloves to the barn, then to school created some interesting snow ball fights. You learn the value of humility when your best friend hits you in the face with a snow ball that has a brown tint to it! When recess was over we would all trudge inside and hang our gloves and mittens on the heating grate to warm and dry. You knew you were in the country when some of those gloves began to bake.

One night a blizzard hit the Emerald area. One of my classmates had a much older sister who was married and had two children. This couple was in Glenwood City when the storm hit, and they tried to make it home despite the storm. They did not make it. The next morning the rescue squad found them by following a trail of discarded clothing. Apparently the advanced stages of hypothermia cause a delusional feeling of being warm, so they shed their clothing. That is enough detail, but I cite this to remind us all that winter in places like Emerald can be a cruel and demanding task master that can punish the foolish.

The blizzard passed. We heard about the gruesome deaths. And that same morning Dad, Irv, and I shoveled snow and then used the sled to haul manure to the field. Life goes on, and it becomes what we make of it. I would not wish for my sons to live the life I did. But, I would not trade one moment of it for anything! Winter was cold. But it was only a momentary coldness on a thermometer. I guess Gogol would not understand me, but this time gave me love and taught me to love, and made it a very warm time in my life.

Chapter 2

Rocks of Ages

My ancestors on both my Father's and Mother's side all came from Ireland. I have always been proud of my Irish ancestry, but whether it is a natural Irish trait or just the specific style of my family, that pride also included a heavy dose of sarcasm, self-deprecation, and even fatalism. I have seen so many people who want to research their ancestry, and God Bless them. But most of them seem to want to find that they are decedents of Tsars, Emperors, or at least came over on the Mayflower with George Washington. (Just a little historical humor, I know George wasn't on the Mayflower) Throw in a Viking warrior or the favorite tart of a randy baron and they are almost giddy.

Many people have asked me if I have any interest in returning to see my ancestral Irish home. I usually say, "No, we have plenty of rocks in Emerald." Usually I just get blank confused stares in return. I know in my heart of hearts that my people left some pile of rocks in west Ireland, and then served as ballast on some leaky ship, and more dead than alive landed on America's east coast. The only 'royal' in our story was the royal screwing the Irish Catholics got at the hands of the British and their 'transplants'. I do know a little history, and that tells me that the British conquest of Ireland was re-enacted by the British colonization of North America. The Indians in America played the role formerly performed by the Irish in Ireland.

We used to say that our ancestors came up the St. Croix River, walked across the county poking a stick in the ground. When they hit enough rocks per square foot, they knew they were home. Ethnic awareness (being politically correct) was a driving force in the 1800's. People of one nationality would find a place to settle and then send for relatives and friends from 'the old country' to this new world. Even when I was born in the mid-1940's people knew that Baldwin was full of Dutch, Woodville had so many Norwegians, Somerset was full of French Canadians, and of course we were the pocket of Irish. I grew up in Emerald Township, which was right next to Erin Prairie Township, and we all went to St. Patrick's Catholic Church. In fact the crossroads of County Rd T and County Rd G is referred to as Erin Corners and it had a combination bar, barbershop and grocery. It was definitely Irish Territory.

In those times a 'mixed marriage' was when you married someone outside your national heritage, and it even got tense if your spouse came from a different parish. I said parish, not different religion. A different religion meant you had 'fallen away' to the forces of hell and perdition, and while some would pray for your return, most simply shook their heads, saying, "And sure 'tis a bad one, 'cuz we lost poor Mary Catherine. Saints be praised!"

The correct response would be, "Oh Jesus Mary and Joseph!"

There were the stories of families literally shunning other family members, and of parents not attending their own child's wedding because of religious or ethnic differences.

There is a line from James A. Michener's "Centennial" that says, "…only the rocks live forever." And I grew up at a time when the 'hard rock attitudes' of the past were starting to change, and change for the better. We now had neighbors with names like Bartnick, Pole (which was actual Pallowitz), Prinsen, and Mikla. Yes, we were proud of being Irish Catholic, but Dad always said if he had to trust his money to anyone it would be Vernie Prinsen. And if Dad could spend time with anyone it might be Walter Pole, who would chew gum constantly to keep his ill-fitting dentures in while he talked. You haven't heard anything as bad as my old Irish Dad trying to mimic a gum-chewing-denture-slopping Polish accent.

We would thrash with John Bartnick, who was as thin and as tough as a piece of barb wire. John also had a Russian-Polish accent, and three teeth. It was always a joke at the thrashing table to see who would offer the other guy a tooth pick. John would offer Walter a tooth pick, so Walter would break it in half and offer the shorter half back to John. Then everyone would laugh. I told you it was a rather happy yet fatalistic group. Most people of this time had no money, poor dental hygiene, and if there was a dentist he was far away and too expensive. Families only went to the dentist on rare occasions, so for many; bad teeth and false teeth were the norm.

Mom made sure Margie and I went to the dentist every year, but I was a married man before I was aware Novocain was an option. I guess it was just accepted that you grab the arm of the dentist chair and gut it out. Even now after 40 years of modern dentistry with 'numbzit' prep followed by Novocain followed by high speed water spray drills I still leave the dentist office with slight cramps in my fingers.

And there, my friends, is a central theme of this wandering diatribe. I have two quotes that run constantly through my life. One I read as a young professional and one was an old Irish expression my Dad used often.

The first quote, heard when I was a young adult, was, "It's not how old you are, it's what it was like when you were young." I wish I could remember who said it so I could now give him credit, but I cannot.

I have tried to tell what it was like in my youth, and I tell of hard work and working hard. I know that millions of young people worked under those conditions or worse. What I am saying is that an old person, a middle aged person and a teenager today could sit down and all tell 'war stories' of similar struggles.

Yes, I would like my sons and grandsons and others to know what I did as a youth. But what fascinates me is that a 90 year old, the teen and I might all have different reactions to the same situations.

I remember reading a book by Theodore H. White called "Breach of Faith: The Fall of Richard Nixon". White notes that Richard Nixon and Hubert H. Humphrey were born two years apart, 1911 and 1913. They both came from lower middle class families, who eventually suffered severe financial crisis. Both boys had to drop out of school to support their families, shattering personal dreams. Both had to settle for 'second class' colleges for their training. Both families suffered terribly during the depression.

Yet Hubert Humphrey grew up "the happy warrior", a liberal who loved life and loves helping people and saw the world as a wonderful place. Richard Nixon became the cynical, bitter, negative person in American politics. Why did this happen? Clearly two separate genetic stocks. Clearly these were two different families with two different environments. But it has to be more than that. I can't explain it, but I use the expression it was two different sets of glasses. I think we all have 'glasses' we wear, and see life through. I know my sister, who shared the same gene pool, shared the same house and same experiences, views her 'life history' different than I do. She remembers 'important things' that I don't even remember, and I remember funny events that she thought were sad.

We all had a great time with lots of love and laughs. And yet she saw our world as different, and here is a silly and yes, embarrassing example.

Margie loved to dress up, have fancy things and celebrate events. Easter to her was a party, with a new Easter dress (usually hand made by Mom) and lots of candy. There was lots of candy because it dawned on me that we all ate Larry's candy first. Then my basket was empty and Margie still had some candy left. I was raised by Lawrence E. and Irvin Moore, with a crazy Uncle Tom (seriously!) and that unholy trio off-set Mom's piety. What would these three do if someone was stealing their candy? No problem! I took my candy behind the sofa and pissed in the basket!

After that my Easter candy, hell my Christmas candy or any other treat lasted until I was damn good and ready to eat it myself!

I put on my set of 'glasses' and saw my world as happy, yet one must protect yourself. For years I was teased about this event, but I had also gained a degree of respect. I will bend and give and compromise on almost everything, especially if it will help others, and 'keep the peace'. But when I pick a point on which I will not budge, God and the Archangels will not move me.

Dad was that way; Irv was that way; and Mom was that way. Mom actually tried to be a saint…or living with us, at least a martyr. She was religious to a fault, she prayed constantly. Mom had more calluses on her knees than all of us had on our hands. God was right; the Pope was right; the Priest was right. Yet I remember so clearly that she often looked at me with wonderful, loving eyes and said, "Larry. God gave you a brain, and he expects you to use it!" This was a woman who was so 'Catholic' that when she had her gall bladder removed, she demanded the surgeon give it to her so she could bury it in St. Patrick's consecrated cemetery, near the unmarked grave of her still-born son. So eventually she was buried whole. And yet again she kept telling me to 'think' and use your brain, even if it challenged existing 'dogma'.

Mom was a public school teacher, and she was great at it, because she not only taught, but also adopted her students. To this day I am not sure whether faith or 'using your brain' were the dominant themes of Mom's life, and thus her influence on me.

Dad. Dad was as unique an individual as was his entrance into this world. Dad was born at home, in the house I grew up in. He weighed 2 pounds, and they put him in a shoe box, and placed him in the cook stove for warmth. We always teased him about being 'half-baked' in more ways than one. Before he was two he had a hernia and chicken pox. But he survived. As he grew, members of his large family died off, some as babies and some as young men or women. He said that over one stretch they wore black for three years straight, because of all the deaths. He was young when his Dad, then his Mother died. So the remaining kids in the house, raised each other. Irv became the 'father' of the family, and Dad never forgot that. Irv was always Irv, but that name also implied a title, and a love that was obvious.

So the second quote that resonates through my life is the old Irish expression, "If you're born to hang, you'll never drown." Dad especially operated on the idea that certain things will happen, and there isn't a damn thing you can do to make it happen or prevent it from happening. So you might as well laugh at fate, and enjoy what you can because 'you play the cards you are dealt'.

Dad worried about the hay, and he worried about the horses, and he worried about how much milk he could get. This he could attempt to control. He really never worried about getting hit by lightning or getting an infection or disease or dying at a certain age. We would get hit by a major Midwest thunder storm, and Mom would have the Blessed candles lit, the Holy Water out, and the Rosary spinning. Dad would be sound asleep in the old rocking chair. Mom would be herding us to the basement, imploring Dad to come with, "Lawrence, it's dangerous outside. We need to go to the basement." Dad would wake up enough to say, "While you're down there, bring me up a Grain Belt." I know this was not bravery, it was not 'bravado', and it was not suicidal. Dad just felt that if it was his time, it didn't matter if he was in the basement or on the roof. And if it wasn't his time, well he needed a nap.

Mom and Dad were the 'rock' of my foundation. I am what I am because of them, and in spite of them. All a parent can do is to do the best they can. I hope my sons gain the best of my history, but I want them to have their own history. One of my truly embarrassing moments as an adult was when I had had way too many beers, and I was pontificating to my wife and friends that "…I had worked, and by God my sons are going to work. Even if I have to force them to carry rocks from one pile to another, they are going to work."

Luckily sobriety and common sense prevailed, and I did not make that mistake. I realized that I could not re-create the work level of my youth, and that if I tried it would be so blatantly obvious that this was 'make work', and thus really a punishment rather than the real work that we had done, the opposite effect would be created. I don't remember ever not working! Yet I don't remember ever 'working' at something stupid. And I honestly don't ever remember ever working at something that wasn't rewarding, and eventually made fun to be fun, by the people I was with.

So often I have mentioned the stages of life, and how age made a transition necessary. It is not how old you are. Dad was born the year before Kitty Hawk, and man's first powered flight. He died after he had flown on a jet, and men had landed on the moon. He was born when a horse could plow a few acres in a day, and died when center pivot tractors could pull plows that turned acres every hour. Dad milked 22 cows, and supplied the farm by horse power, and before he died exactly two miles from his farm a corporate farm was milking 1700 cows and they were fed by 18-wheelers bringing in high quality feed from all over America.

I feel so lucky because I was able to share in this monumental change period. I was able to work a farm in a manner that was relatively unchanged for hundreds of years, and now it changes so fast I honestly feel I never farmed.

We fed good alfalfa, and the top cows got a coffee can full of grain on top of their bucket of silage. Today, computers dominate most farms, tracking the futures market, crop prices and bids, and the food ration and milk production of each cow.

But what I have learned is that life is about people. I don't care if they are immigrants, poor rock-soil farmers, or high tech Agri-business farmers.

Many of Mom's and Dad's everyday expressions and attitudes are still ringing in my head today. In fact many of them cut through modern techno-talk and make more sense than ever. Look at the grid-lock in modern government or business or education, and Dad would remind us that "…a small team pulling together…" would be best. I look at these huge mega-corporations and the stock market fluctuations, and I remember Dad spending $1.25 on his total harvest cost. He often said, "It's not how much you earn, it's how much you keep."

But back to people, because, I feel, we have lost the empathy, the love for people in this world. Complete factories are closed down, and hundreds are laid off. We call that 'down sizing' and the lives of real people become a statistic.

My teaching was always about the totality of history and life not just the events and dates. I may have jeopardized my title of teacher, the last years of my teaching career because I was so busy helping people. Now contractually that was wrong, because I was hired to teach History, I was not hired to be everyone's personal guidance counselor. But I was raised by Mary Moore, who so often said, "If you are not helping, what good are you?" Yes, maybe I had rocks in my head, but I spent many years of my teaching career fighting for students and teachers. This was not the straight teaching the administration wanted; I was not strictly doing the job I was hired for. But what could I do? I think I was helping to create well rounded, centered, young adults. I could no more ignore a plea for help than I could say, "Hell it's too cold for me…you go to the barn!"

I feel some sadness, but mainly an overwhelming sense of pride when I think of my sons. More than once each of them has taken a 'shot' because they stood for something that only they thought was right. I hope some day they read this and know how much I love them, and how proud I am of them. And if necessary, I apologize for being a Moore. (Cue the sarcasm.)

So often I use the rock analogy. But it works for me. To me a rock is stable and predictable and unmoving and constant. My formative years were full of rocks. Not cold and unemotional rocks but happy and loving rocks.

I still remember Irv. Irv did not get old as he aged, he just changed jobs. When Irv went to the rest home he aged, because he no longer had his job. Getting older isn't so much a date on the calendar or a slower, stooped walk. Being old is a sense of not being important any more.

Dad and Irv no longer farmed. Dad and Irv had aged.

Irv died on April 27, 1977.

Dad died on April 27, 1978.

Exactly one year later.

I think they just missed each other!

Chapter 3

The Holy Trinity of Farming

I hope no one is offended by this mixed metaphor of religion and farming, but with my Irish Catholic upbringing if I can't make a little fun of two of the dominant forces in my life, well who can? You see, Dad was the farmer and Mom was only slightly less Catholic than the Bishop, so it seems like a natural blend.

Plus Dad had a natural mixture of sarcasm, humor, and Irish fatalism that still rings in my ears as much as Mom's spirituality challenges my emotions. So these are my recollections about farm life in Emerald. Notice I said recollections, not facts. What I am writing are my personal memories of events in the earliest days of my life. While I will attempt to be honest and true, I feel comfortable with the knowledge that some of my facts will turn out to not be facts and some of my stories might be doubted by those of a critical nature.

Mom taught me never to lie, for that was a sin. Dad occasionally sat with the truth, but he really loved to dance with a story. In a typical Irish way, Dad had more fun telling the story than making a point. In fact, I think Dad's favorite means of conversation was to let it be known right away that he was lying...ahem... embellishing the story. Even today my wife gets frustrated with me when I tell a joke. She will say, "You never tell the same joke the same way twice!" Hey, that keeps me interested because even I don't know how I am going to get to the end, and when I do this 'new joke' is even funny to me.

The Holy Trinity of Farming for the Moore family was oats, alfalfa, and corn. Any money that came from the farm mainly came from the cattle, which could be milked, sold as adults or sold as calves, but it was the Holy Trinity that kept all the animals alive. Chickens, turkeys, and pigs were a minor source of money, but mainly supplied a source of food for the table, and the horses supplied most of the muscle to work the farm. I suppose it was a 'dairy farm' but I have never been comfortable with that term. Our farm did have a dairy aspect, but it really was a very low-tech high-labor self-sufficiency operation.

Yes, it was low-tech. Yes, it was high-labor. Maybe self-sufficient is an over-statement, but not by much. As I said before, I remember one fall when all the planting and harvesting was complete, Dad proudly announced that we had spent $1.25 on equipment that season. One sickle guard on the hay mower was all we had to buy. All the rest came from the farm itself. I must clarify that we did buy some quality alfalfa seed, our corn seed and fertilizer. Yes, and Dad did give Mom some cash to buy extra groceries for the thrashing crew, but I think we broke even on that because of all the times we ate at other farms.

I can still hear Dad saying, "A continual round of pleasure". It didn't take long to figure out this was his sardonic way of saying that the cycle never stops. The cycle was to haul it to the field as seed; harvest it as a crop; feed it to the animals; then haul it back to the field as manure to fertilize next years seed.

It was never-ending, low-tech high-labor …but I guess I am one of the lucky ones, because working with my Dad and my Uncle Irv (my second dad), were also some of the most rewarding and fun days of my life. It was long, hard work, and I did often envy my 'town friends' who were playing ball or fishing or any of a hundred things I felt they were getting away with while I was working my ass off. But we laughed. We had fun. We actually enjoyed being around each other. I know it is over used, but I was loved. It was hardly ever said, but you just knew it because it was that obvious.

I remember many times Mom would be calling Dad, and Mary would be calling Irv to come in for supper. They would be calling repeatedly because Dad and Irv were there, surrounded by night, standing under a dim yard light, talking like they hadn't seen each other for years. Usually not one word of sense would take place. Dad would be spinning some tale, and Irv would be grinning like he had never heard this before. Then the ladies would call again, sometimes flipping the yard light off and on to emphasize the message. Dad would grin and say, "Murtha's" and Irv would grin back saying, "Dean's" and that would end the conversation.

The trouble with explaining each member of the 'Trinity' is where do you start explaining? Oats for example would be harvested in the fall, but the same oats would be used as seed oats in the spring. I guess I will start with the worst and get it out of the way. Even as I write, I get the 'skin-crawling shivers' thinking about oats. I absolutely hate oat's dust. Chewing aluminum foil or getting slivers under my finger nails would cause me less trauma compared to dealing with oat dust.

The worst was fanning oats. In late winter we would go to the grainery. Yes, I learned in school it is spelled granary, but in Emerald it was grainery just like the tiny flowing waterway is pronounced 'crick'. I don't care if the map spells it creek, and that Dry Run Creek ran through our land, it was a 'crick'. So my computer spell check will run out of red ink reminding me that grainery is not a word, but I still say we did not go into the fields to harvest gran! And when we got thirsty we didn't drink Gran Belt Beer.

See what oats can do to me? Even after all these years, oats can still get me in a fighting mood.

Late spring was often cold, and of course there was no heat in the grain…oh, hell, in the grain storage building! Ha! This building had six storage units, with two bigger units upstairs, and four smaller ones occupying the four corners of the lower unit, with a hallway and stairs separating the four lower units. In the fall, grain would be blown into the upstairs units (more on this at another time) and as they filled, the grain would be pushed through one of four holes in the floor into one of the corresponding rooms on the lower floor. As these rooms filled, board after board would be added to the inside of the doorway, with the weight of the oats keeping the boards in place. This made a door that could be opened six inches at a time by removing one board after another.

Can you imagine the dust? Can you imagine the sweat and the dust? Can you wait until I go shower?

So now in late spring we would awaken 'the monster' which still gives me nightmares. We just called it 'the fan' and the process we called 'fanning oats'. Don't let the simplicity of the words fool you, it was hell on earth.

The fan was a cube of about four feet by four feet by four feet. It consisted on a series of vertically stacked screens that were exposed to a hand-cranked wooden slatted fan at the rear. The fan would be cranked and oats from the bin would be shoveled in the top. The crank turned the fan, and as it did it also caused the screens to slide back and forth, each screen in the opposite direction of the screen above it. The screens would slide and bounce, shaking seeds as the fan made a wind force. Seeds smaller than the desired oat size would fall through the screens, seeds larger would be trapped, and seeds that were the desired size would be in one screen box. And the hateful dust would be blown off the seed.

Winnowing gran (ha, I am still bitter!) is as old as the Bible, so our low-tech method sure improved on using a stick, a blanket and the wind. Now instead of taking days to winnow, and days of being dirty this could all be compressed into two wonderful hours. Now several days worth of dust could be pounded into your hair, ears, eyes, nose and any other orifice not covered by layers of protection in a matter of hours. Ah, progress!

I am going to skip several obvious steps, like spring arrives. I am going to skip plowing, disking, dragging, and go directly to planting. Needless to say the soil must be prepared, but just as important the ground must be warm enough. How did you determine this? An old friend and the father of one of my students, told me he had a neighbor who wore bib overalls… now hang on, this is my story, and I will tell it the Irish way! The bibs are important, because this old farmer would go out into the fields in the spring and sit on the prepared land. He would sit and smoke a pipe full. When the pipe was done, he would stand up and consider his butt situation. If it was too wet or too cold he would not plant.

Now I warned you earlier about validity issues, but this old friend was a man who usually told the truth, so I am sticking to his story.

My earliest memories of planting oats involved getting out the drill. It seemed like another monster to a child but it was probably only twelve feet across. It had wooden wheels with iron bands around the outer parts. There were two storage bins for the oat seeds, and two smaller ones for the alfalfa seeds. The oats and alfalfa seeds were planted at the same time. The quick growing oats was considered a cover crop for the slower growing alfalfa. As the drill was pulled the wheels turned, thus causing an auger to force seeds out of the boxes and down metal tubes into the soil. Metal disks then covered the seed with dirt.

The main power source for all of this work was our horses. The Moore farm was all about horses for a very long time. My grandfather at one time had 24 horses on the farm, some for personal use and many to sell or trade. In my youth we always had at least two horses, and Dad was partial to Belgians. Dad was a good man, and also a very good horseman. He knew how to handle them, but he was also considerate of his horses, never mistreating them.

Pulling a large drill through freshly worked soil for hours was hard work. If we only had two horses Dad would barter the use of two more horses from one of the neighbors. That way he could use three or four horses to share the pull. Another benefit of this system was to put a young, inexperienced and often skittish horse in the middle, with two experienced horses flanking the two-year old. Dad never considered working anything under two years old, as he felt their bones and muscles were still soft. Sandwich a youngster with 1800 pounds of trained muscle on each side, pull for 3 hours over soft soil, and by the end of planting you usually had a very cooperative young horse.

If Dad had four experienced horses, he would stop every hour or two (depending on the temperature) and rotate the inside horses to the outside where it would be cooler. We also had a collection of woven-mesh fly nets to drape over the horses, and some metal nose guards in case the biting flies were bad. But the flies would have to be real bad because Dad felt the nets and especially the nose guards made it hotter and more miserable for the horses than it already was.

Dad was the horseman, but he did let me try my hand at seeding. The trick was to follow the wheel track in the fresh soil. If you planted in a north-south manner, you made two tracks on your first north-south passage. At the end of the field you had to pull the left horse back, while getting the right horse to swing ahead and around. This would pivot the drill around so that the left wheel of the drill would now cover the track in the soil from the left wheel on your first pass.

The driver would ride on a little platform on the right side of the drill on one pass, watching the right wheel follow the track. At the end of the pass he would have to pivot the team and drill, then jump off the right platform, run over and jump up on the similar left platform in time to line the left wheel up with the left track. Over and over this rotation would take place at each end of the field. So the driver is holding multiple lines, watching tracks, and jumping for side to side at the end of each pass. He was a driver, not a rider.

The oats was the first part of the Holy Trinity. But oats was what was called a 'cover crop'. Yes, we did use the oats for next year's seed, and yes we did feed some of the oats. But the main function of the oats was to aid in the development of the alfalfa crop. Oats would germinate in several days. It would hold the soil together, and provide shade and shelter for the slowly emerging alfalfa crop. The oats would be harvested, but most people miss the fact that oats were removed so it did not impede the growth of the alfalfa. This was actually as important as the quality and value of the grain. Oats gave you more oats, it gave your alfalfa cover, and it gave you wonderful straw for bedding your animals.

But alfalfa made you a famer, and alfalfa made you money! Dad always said it was alfalfa that made this country. Before alfalfa, what farmers grew was just grass. Ok, I am not a botanist or modern agri-businessman so I am not even going to try to explain nutrition with any high tech explanations. What I know is what Dad told me, and he said, that when he was young the food value of what they could harvest would just barely help keep the cows alive during the long winter. You could only handle a few cows because of the volume and quality of the grasses that could be harvested. Most farmers "dried up" (did not milk) their cows during the winter months, because a cow could not make milk, and survive, on the poor quality of food that was available for them.

It was the introduction of alfalfa to this area that changed farming forever. Under normal conditions alfalfa could produce a crop that was high in protein and food value for cattle. Again, under normal conditions alfalfa was a renewable crop, usually producing a crop for the farmer for at least five years. Farmers counted on getting multiple harvests each year, with three crops not out of the ordinary. Now farmers counted on full hay mows with high quality hay through the winter. Herd size could increase, and the milking days could be extended. Now the farmer could not only provide for his family's needs of milk, cream, and butter but he could count on a surplus which could be sold for profit. Border-line self-sufficiency was getting nudged by the possibility of actual profit.

This transformation is so subtle that most people, including some farmers miss the impact of alfalfa. Before this, calves and pigs often fended for themselves in straw piles, and some people actually fed swamp grass to their horses....just enough to keep them alive. The expression 'horse hay' is still in many peoples vocabulary. It was food for the horse, but it was far from being good nourishing alfalfa hay.

Dad often told the story about working a deal with a northern lumber company. Dad kept two horses home, and then took the rest to Cylon where they were put on a train and shipped north to the lumber camp for the winter. The lumber company got free horse power for the winter, and the Moore's kept their horses alive during the winter. The lumber camp would close for the summer so Dad got back well fed horses for the spring planting season.

Actually what he got back were monsters! There were two things that happened in any lumber camp...you worked and you ate. That was true for men, and that was true for animals. These horses would work all day pulling heavy logs around the forest, but they would get the best grain and hay. They would come back to Emerald in the best shape of their lives. After pulling heavy logs over uneven ground covered with snow, pulling our 'monster' grain drill was like a walk in the pasture. Worse yet, to get a log to move the horse learned to explode against the weight to get it started, and then pull like crazy until the task was done. Imagine that much muscle exploding against a grain drill and sprinting to the end of the field! Their newly learned style would either kill the driver or wreck the equipment, so Dad felt that logging and farming really did not mix.

I can measure my early growth and development by haying. Without looking for pity, I do not ever remember not working, and this was especially true during the haying season. My earliest memories were of hauling either a Mason jar or a bottle of Grain Belt to the barn for Dad and Irv. No, I did not get a drink because I had not worked.

My first real job was as the 'trip man' on the hay fork, and I will cover this later. Then there was the real man's job of driving the team while the load of hay was being built. It was a wonderful and sad transition as I grew up that my beloved Irv got old, and I took over more and more of his tasks. But it was the typical extended family where the young move into tasks as the older move on to other tasks. Until the day Irv went to the rest home, he always had a job on the farm. I still think he really started to die when he stopped working. But the greater joys are the stories we can tell of work shared, lies told, and the great fun of both.

The first step in harvesting alfalfa is cutting it, which is called mowing. Our mower was an old John Deere horse drawn side-cutter. Crudely explained, the mower was all steel. Steel wheels, steel seat, steel mechanism, and steel cutting blade. Basically as the horses pulled the mower forward, the gears caused the 'sickle' to slice back and forth, thus cutting the alfalfa. The faster the horses walked the fast the sickle sliced. This was often a problem because if the horses walked too fast through thick alfalfa the sickle would jam up with more than it could cut.

The sickle blade was about five feet long, with a wooden 'mold board' at the end, with a protruding stick bracketed at an upward angle from this board. The purpose of this was to force the outer edge of mowed alfalfa back onto the rest of the cut hay. This made a clear and obvious 'part' which showed the end of one cut and the place to begin on the next round. This clearly showed each round but more importantly kept a clear space so the sickle did not get jammed up on the next round.

One of my lasting impressions of haying was how quiet it was. The noise of mowing hay was the sound of two horses walking. The sickle did make a sound of metal on metal, a quiet clack-clack-clack. Dad never spared the grease, so the whole mower was remarkably quiet.

The overwhelming and lasting memory of haying is the smell. Even today while driving a car 55 miles per hour down a highway, the smell of new mown hay is overwhelming and causes a collage of thoughts and memories. In actual time the smells were more graphic and immediate. Yes, there were the wonderful smells of new mown alfalfa. I can smell it now. There was also the smell of sweat from two 1800 pound Belgians. And unless you are a 'horse person' you do not know the amount of gas that a fully functioning horse can produce.

Here is an image. You are sitting on a steel seat on a steel mower. The seat is located within a few feet of your horse power. You are basically eye-to-anus with your beloved power source. On a calm day a driver will fully be sharing in the dietary by-products of a Belgian. Now in the scope of the universe, this is insignificant. Ask any old farm hand how long a Belgian fart can last! The old expression "…and time stood still…" takes on new meaning!

The hay is cut, so now it must be raked. The purpose of raking is to get most of the hay off the ground so it can dry quickly without losing the 'greenness' of its leaves. That is where the main food value is, so if it gets too dry too quick or is handled roughly, all the leaves can be knocked off, thus reducing the nutritional value of the hay tremendously.

My dad used a 'side delivery rake' when I was a little child. Before that came the dump rake, and if you are a farm lover you know what that is. If you don't know about it, good for you because it is work beyond work times four! The side delivery rake is a system of four long rotating metal bars, each containing steel wire tongs that point down-wards. As the horse pulls the rake the four bars rotate, and the tongs scoops the hay off the ground, constantly moving it sideways and forward. This makes what is called a 'windrow'. This keeps the hay off the ground, sitting on the stubble of the cut hay. This way it can dry and still retain the important leaves. A horse drawn rake makes even less noise than a horse drawn mower. About all you hear are horse footsteps and the constant 'whish-whish-whish' of the rotating rake bars.

Hay cut, hay raked, but now comes the hard part. Is the hay fit to be put in the hay mow? If the hay is too dry you risk losing all the food value. If the hay is too wet it will be miserable to handle, which is the least of the problem. Wet hay packed inside a closed container may spontaneously combust. We did not have to be chemists to respect the real possibility of barn fires. Even today I do not completely understand spontaneous combustion but I do remember visiting neighbors who lost everything because of a hay fire. When I grew up most farmers would openly state they would rather lose their house than their barn, so putting up bad hay was always a danger. It was delicate because too early was dangerous, and too late was worthless.

It usually took until midday for the hay to be ready to load. So almost always we would load hay after dinner.

And by the way, dinner was the meal that real Americans ate at 12:00…which is noon. This is just a little personal aside, but dinner is at noon. Pronounce it differently it becomes diner, as in diner's club. Fine, but lots of people can go to a diner at any time of day. But a supper club is only open in the evening. Dinner = noon meal. Supper = late day meal. That is a rule in Emerald. Final argument is that Jesus Christ did not have a 'last dinner' but he sure had a 'Last Supper'.   I just think I've got the Pope and Mary Moore on this one, so I declare myself the winner!

Bringing the hay in from the field was also a low-tech, high-labor operation. The raking process piled the mown hay into long rows of fluffy hay that sat on top of the alfalfa stubble, and that made it easier to lift off the ground. Before my time, men walking on foot would use three-tined hay forks to pick up the hay. In my youth we had advanced to using a machine simply called the hay loader.

The hay loader would be attached to the back of the hay wagon, usually by a U-shaped clevis. The horses would pull the wagon which of course then caused the loader to move. The loader rolled on steel wheels, and the two large rear wheels turned gears which caused a series of vertical ropes and horizontal slats to move in a continuous forward and upward motion. The team of horses walked forward, the windrow of hay between them. The windrow would pass under the wagon, and between the wagon tires until it got to the loader. The loader slats would catch the fluffy yet entwined hay and feed it up the slats until it went over the top of the loader and onto the wagon. As the hay landed on the wagon a man would use his 3-tined pitch fork to move the hay to various parts of the wagon. This was called 'building the load' and it took a certain skill to stack a large amount of fairly slippery hay into a unit that stayed on the wagon, a wagon with a front and back but no sides, a load that was big enough in volume to make the trip to the field worthwhile.

And now pride, skill, and seniority on the Moore farm came into play. When Dad was young and in his prime he would often go to the field by himself. Well, he and his horses, Maude and Jim. Maude and Jim were his pride and joy. Even late in his life he would get kind of emotional talking about them, and end the conversation with some wise-ass sarcasm about dumb horses. I never knew what happened to this team, and very early I just knew not to ask.

When heading to the hay field Dad could tie the harness lines to the wagon, and lay down on the wagon for a short nap. Maude and Jim knew how to get to the field. When they arrived at the right spot they would stop, and Dad would wake up. I know there were times when he wasn't asleep, but I know he was just enjoying the feeling of pride in these fine animals.

Sometimes it was a two-man operation, and for a while Irv had seniority so he drove the team while Dad built the load. Those two would be talking and 'arguing' during the whole process, each claiming that it was his skill that made the load a quality operation, and that they would be done already if the other wasn't slowing things down.

At a very early age I earned the right to go to the field. I was just big enough to do man's work, and of course dress like a man and talk like a man. My first job was to just walk around, staggering on the moving wagon to help pack the load down on the wagon. In retrospect I am sure this had no real value, but it was part of my rite of passage. Besides, I gave Dad and Irv a new victim to tease.

As I got older I was given the opportunity to drive the team. I was an incredibly skilled horseman from the very beginning, but again in retrospect I do remember being told to hold the lines so loose and slack that I now know the team was really driving themselves. Any time the field got hilly or we came to the end of the windrow, it seemed like it was now Irv's turn to drive.

As we all aged, Irv retired to jobs in the barn like oiling pulleys and braiding ropes. I became a real driver while Dad loaded. And when I was 'man enough' Dad rotated to driving while I built the load. My first load was a masterpiece. At least until we hit a small side-hill and most of the load slid off the wagon and back onto the ground. Dad stopped the team and looked at me with great seriousness and said, "Interesting plan. I usually unload in the barn." I was given the reward of building that load a second time while Dad was busy repairing a suddenly discovered flaw in the harness. Luckily the harness repair was completed just as I finished picking up the last stem of alfalfa.

For the rest of the load all I heard was Dad 'talking to himself' about how it was hard finding good help; that he had heard that that McGee boy up the road was a great load builder, and he was German; and maybe my sister Margie could drive the team....ya, she was a damn fine driver...and how he, even in his advancing age might have to go back to building loads.

I built the best load in my life, or so I prayed. I almost placed the hay stem by stem so it wouldn't fall and that the load would be as square as a box. I prayed like a sinner right before entering the confessional that this load would be perfect, and that Dad would not tell Irv.

God must have been busy that day because the load was not great, and Irv got to hear the whole story. In fact Irv got to hear details that did not happen, and could not have happened. All day I kept hearing from Dad and Irv about how they would like to be done haying before the first snow.

I think I was one of the first people to have stereo. My stereophonic sound center played non-stop teasing, lying, sarcasm, and outright 'bovine droppings'. Irv on one side, Dad on the other; these two speakers played some interesting 'music' in my youth. What can I say, I was an abused child. Luckily I was not impacted by any of this, and grew up to be a fine and stable man. This gene is apparently a dominant gene because my wife and boys often roll their eyes at my stories and now our sons show the signs of inheriting this trait of dry humor, teasing, and subtle sarcasm.

Eventually the load of hay is brought in from the field to the barn. The specific part of the barn for the hay is the hay mow. Our barn sat north-south at its length, with the east side having an earthen ramp that led up to the hay mow. This ramp was at mid-barn and it led to two huge sliding doors that opened into a huge passageway. When the doors were opened we could drive the team and hay wagon right into the middle of the barn. The team would then be unhitched from the wagon and led one at a time between the wagon and the hay already stacked in the mow. If the mow was full and the wagon load was large it was an interesting experience leading an 1800 pound horse out through this 'hay tunnel'. You would have to duck and run to keep ahead of a plunging horse on a short check rein.

Once the horses were out they were re-hitched to each other, and one horse was connected to a 'single-tree'. Two chains, one on each side of the horse's harness were connected to a stout piece of wood. This wood piece had a hook and clevis system that was connected to the hay rope. This large hay rope was fed through a series of pulleys up to the hay track that spanned the very top of the barn. It was this system of ropes, pulleys, and track that allowed us to unload the hay from the wagon and transport it into the mow for storage.

A smaller trip rope would be used to pull the carrier (which rolled on the ceiling track) to the middle of the barn. Once in the middle there was a trip system that allowed the large hay fork to be lowered onto the load. This larger fork came in three styles, depending on the quality of hay and the amount you want to off-load each time. There was a harpoon fork which consisted of one single tine. This tine would be pushed down into the hay, and then a lever would be pulled at the top causing two smaller projections to lever out of the bottom tip of the harpoon. These projections would catch hay and the tine would pull the hay up to the carrier. Upon hitting the carrier a trip lever would allow the load to roll either north or south into the mow. The smaller trip rope would be pulled, forcing the two projectiles back into the shaft of the harpoon, and gravity would cause the hay to drop down.

The two other forks were a double tined fork and a four tined grapple fork, but they basically work on the same principle as the harpoon fork. The one advantage was that the double tined fork carried double the single tined, and the four tined fork carried double the double tined. These Moore's, are they good at math or what?

Again, the seniority system came into play. As a child I carried water to the men. My first promotion was to stand behind the wagon, but away from the pulley system, and hold the trip rope. Just hold the rope, let it easily slip through your hands, and just keep it from getting caught on anything. Then Dad or Irv would take it, give it a yank and cause the hay to drop. If you tripped it too soon, the hay would fall back down on the wagon, and the whole effort was wasted. If you tripped it too late, all the hay would land in one pile, and make more work for the man in the mow. But if you could time it just right, when the load was still rolling on the track, the hay would be dropped the whole length of the mow. Perfect!

I learned one lesson very quickly. Wear leather gloves! As that hemp rope was being dragged through your hands the friction could literally blister your hands. And you definitely did not want to get hemp slivers. As my work assignments changed the sweat level increased. I found leather gloves to be hot, but that was off-set by the protection they gave. And as a bonus, wet leather gloves made griping leather harness lines and wood handled forks much easier.

Age caused a rotation of jobs. Irv needed to come out of the mow, so Dad did both the fork setting and spreading the hay in the hay mow. Irv ran the trip rope, and helped with the pulley ropes. I graduated to driving the fork horse. This was the horse with the single tree connected to the large hay rope. Once Dad set the fork and got safely back into the mow, I would drive the fork horse.

The horse learned quickly that this load could be heavy, so to get it started the horse would hit with a starting lunge. He would have to pull for about 40 feet, usually lunging all the way. Now it became tricky, because the horse needed momentum plus strength to get the load up to the carrier. Once the fork hit the track carrier a trip lever released the carrier, sending it into the mow. I had to make sure the horse kept lunging until the fork hit the carrier, and then, almost immediately, stop the horse. If he kept pulling he could smash the load right through the end of the barn. Not good. If he stopped too soon he would not have the strength and momentum to finish the pull, so the trip man would have to trip the load to save the horse from injury or wrecking the whole pulley system. Also not good.

A good horse would start the load with a lunge, take the bit in his teeth, and keep pulling. I learned to trust most of our horses so rather than try to make my short little legs run down the ramp behind him, I would hold the lines tight, lean back, and let the horse drag me down the ramp. I think I invented 'dirt surfing' about that time. Most of our horses learned that when the fork hit the carrier, the load would lighten, and they would stop on their own. But you just couldn't count on that. Besides, once the pull was over the driver had to unhook the end of the hay rope from the single tree, hold the single tree in one hand, and using the other hand turn the horses around so they could walk back up the ramp for the next load. Again with one hand full of single tree the team had to be turned around. Irv would have pulled the large rope back by then, so he would re-hook it while Dad re-set the fork. Yup, a continual round of pleasure.

When the last hay was off the wagon the horses were tied to the north side of the silo for safety. This was necessary because the empty wagon had to be pushed out of the mow, and down the ramp. The key job was holding and guiding the wagon tongue, which was the pole that was used by the horses to help pull and steer the wagon. Once we got the wagon started down the ramp momentum took over. This made the pushing unnecessary but now you had a run-away wagon to deal with. If you could run fast enough while holding and steering the tongue you could avoid having the wagon crash into something or flip because the front wheels turned too sharply.

Break time. Irv would tidy up the alley between the two mows. Dad would take a pencil and mark down the number of this load. On one of the beams he would make one vertical mark with his pencil; four vertical lines, then one diagonal slash meant five loads in the barn. Every spring Dad would write the year on a beam, and then record the number of loads that year. Each spring he would write the month and year on the inside of the grain drill, and the number of loads of hay in the barn. Now we are talking low-tech record keeping here!

Load after load would go into the barn in this manner. Cutting, raking, and loading based on horse and man power to set the pace. And of course personality entered the equation. Dad wanted quality hay, he would be so proud of how many loads he could get in the barn without it being touched by a drop of rain. He took it as a personal challenge to balance the harvest against nature, taking it as a personal insult if any of his hay got wet. He would go out after dinn….the noon meal…smile…and check the hay.

He would feel it, he would smell it, and he would twist it trying to determine if it was ready for his barn.

More than once I remember the three of us loading hay in the field, with an obvious storm approaching. You never whip a horse, but they would be talked into picking up the pace. The faster the pace the faster the hay was fed up the loader the more furiously we built the load. This hay was not going to get wet, so damn the lightning! So here we were, the tallest thing in an open field, two of us holding metal tipped forks, trying to out-run nature over one load of hay. Brilliant!

If I were a good writer I could infuse this tale with all the drama, thrills, and excitement worthy of a Michener or a Grisham. But in my minds eye I can claim that this passed for high drama and low comedy in Emerald.

The load was built. Unhitch the loader. Head for the barn. Into the mow went horses and wagon. Unhitch the team and lead them through the hay tunnel, and head straight for the horse barn door. I would lead while Dad started to unharness the horses as they walked. Irv would be closing the hay mow doors. Horses safe, hay safe we would run for the house…and not make it! The rain would come down in buckets, and we would stop and just stand there. We couldn't get any wetter, so you might as well laugh.

We didn't need to worry about the lightning because by now Mom had cracked opened the Holy Water jar, and was going through the beads on the Rosary like the teeth on a running chain saw.

So with trying to hide the smiles on our faces, we would dutifully promise not to be that foolish again, and not get the floor wet. We would take off most of our clothes on the big front porch, and then I would be sent to the basement to get our reward. Dad always kept a case of beer in the basement. Basement temperature Grain Belt or Leinekugels were the beers of choice. Most of the time we shared one bottle, two at the most. I do not ever remember being 'old enough' to have a full bottle of beer while on the farm. Irv was given a glass, because he loved to tap a little salt into the beer.

An occasional beer and Christmas and Easter wine were allowed (after saying Grace) but rarely anything stronger. And the wine was a small bottle from that famous Irishman Mogan David.

Like any good Irish story we have traveled from haying to lightning storms to the consumption of spirits. Stay with me because this will all make sense, all in its own good time!

You see, our land adjoined the Kennedy farm. Patrick, Margaret Ellen, and Miles Kennedy, now there was a three-some. As they used to say, they were as Irish as Paddy's pig and damn proud of it. I know they had some money, but they rarely spent it…and especially on wages. Most of the time neighbors would barter labor for labor, equipment for equipment. But occasionally someone would have to be hired for a task. Well the Kennedy's never paid in cash. They paid in alcohol. Now it was good quality beer and whiskey, not some home-made swill. There is quality and there is quality in this world, and the Kennedy's drew that line at the tavern door.

If you worked for the Kennedy's you might earn a beer. You might work long enough for a six pack. A short but energetic job may earn a swig or two out of the whiskey bottle. If Dad helped he would always take a beer or two, sometimes drinking it there but often bringing one home. If the pay was whiskey a certain protocol was followed. Miles Kennedy always paid, that was his pride. Dad really didn't like the taste of whiskey, but was honor bound to accept payment. So he would tip the bottle up and take one big long swig, give the required 'ahhhh' and return the bottle. I witnessed this with my own eyes on several occasions.

One day Dad, and young me helped Miles move some cattle from one farm to another. Miles was 'modern' so he had a tractor, I can still see that Farmal H. His tractor pulled a wagon full of fresh cut hay down the road. Dad and I walked behind the cattle to keep them controlled, but most of the cattle just followed the hay wagon, trying to steal something to eat.

Once the cattle arrived at the new pasture, and were safely fenced in, Miles was ready to pay. So he took a big swig, and then gave it to Dad. Dad did his ritual. The bottle was then capped and thrown up onto the hay wagon. On the return trip Dad stood on the back of the tractor so he could talk to Miles. I rode on the hay wagon by myself. Using a child's sense of logic, I felt I had worked so I deserved to be paid just like Dad. After all, a man is a man when he does man's work. So I grabbed the old whiskey bottle, unscrewed the cap, and took a little pull. Well I intended to take a little pull, but just then the wagon hit a bump, and I shot what felt like twelve gallons of whiskey down my throat.

Oh Sweet Jesus, I thought I was going to die! My throat burned; my stomach was on fire; my tongue lost movement; my eyes shed tears, lost focus, and spun in their sockets. I thought I was going to throw up…I prayed I could throw up. I wanted to scream for Dad, but I didn't want Dad to know what I had done. It felt like that tractor was in slow motion, I couldn't get home quick enough. Now I had to figure out how to gracefully and secretly get off the wagon and away from Dad.

Like an old elephant I wanted to just wander off alone to die. No luck. Dad saw me and asked what was wrong. A quick check of the Ten

Commandments did not say specifically one could not tell a white lie, but I did have to honor my father, so without baring false witness I told him the truth. To my surprise he broke out in laughter.

First, he was fine with my logic about getting paid.

Second, he thought I had learned a lesson about strong drink.

Third, he told me how he was able to drink so much of Miles' whiskey. You stick your tongue in the bottle hole so none comes out. Damn him!

When the haying was done, we moved on to harvesting the oats. Late in the fall we would harvest the corn. Again, both were low-tech high-labor operations. I am not sure it benefits either the reader or the writer to go into details on every crop and every harvest. Both the oats and the corn were cut with reapers that left bundles on the ground, and these bundles had to be stacked. These stacks give a rather idealistic and iconic picture to farming, with the traditional Halloween stacks or the romantic image of the fields of oat or wheat stacks.

I could wax poetic about harvest time, and present it through the nimbus of golden years of times long past. I do have wonderful memories of all of this, and the memories are all brought into sharp focus by the counter-balance of incredibly long hard days of labor. So I will exercise the author's privilege and move on to a different topic.

Horses are so much a part of this story, and the whole Moore experience. Many people who shared a similar past have different and varied emotions and memories concerning horses. Even my Dad who truly loved his horses had no time for the kind you ride. Horses meant work horses. Any other horse just took up space and wasted good food. Late in his life he still would not attend horse pulls because he felt that they wrecked a good horse. He could be a hazard on the highway if he drove past a field with work horses in it, but wouldn't even turn his head if they were 'ponies'. All non-work horses were ponies to him.

We had horses that worked and earned their keep, and also earned Dad's undying respect and love. We had one Belgian-Clydesdale mix that was Dad's kind of horse. One day on a trip to the Cylon feed mill to get raw grain milled, Dad had Laddie weighed. He came in at a little over 2100 pounds. His feet were as big as pie pans. You could set a checker board on his back and I swear the board would lay flat. As a boy trying to throw a harness on him was like throwing a harness on the roof of the barn. And he was as gentle and docile as a teddy bear.

I remember one time I was trying to harness him, and I literally threw part of the harness like a fisherman casting a net, hoping part of the harness would reach the opposite side. I did not have to bend much to pass right under him rather than walk around, where I would jump up to try and catch the thrown part of the harness. Just as I landed Laddie picked up his front foot and shifted slightly, with his huge hoof landing right on the tip of my shoe.

Luckily all he got was leather. Had he landed on my foot he would have smashed every bone in that foot. He was totally unaware that he had pinned my shoe, but I was now trapped. I was really in no danger, but I was frustrated and embarrassed to be pinned to the ground by a horse I was supposed to be harnessing. I am not proud of this next sequence, but what the hell…I will probably be dead by the time someone reads this. Anyway, being young and brilliant I tried shoving Laddie over! Remember, 2100 pounds and I am going to push him aside. Ok, it gets worse because I tried picking up his leg. This would be approximately similar to lifting a telephone post. Next logical step was to reach down and grab his hairy fetlock in an attempt to just lift his foot. Like that is going to work! Now loosing whatever dignity I may have retained I started slapping, then pounding on his shoulder. I am sure he thought I was patting him for being a good boy for standing so still.

I was seriously considering removing my shoe at this time, because I was not going to call out for Dad or Irv. They had plenty of ammunition with which to tease me as it was, so I was not going to provide them with more. Eventually Laddie raised his massive head out of the manger, and turned to look at me. He shifted and moved his foot and I was released. If I didn't know better I would swear he had held me on purpose, and had enjoyed a great little horse humor. And based on my actions, I am still not sure who the 'dumb animal' in this story was.

The first team I remember driving were Pete and Tilley. Yes, I swear they were Pete and Tilley. Of course they were Dad's team and he used them the most, but I did get to use them a lot. Most of my youth was spent working with Duke and Bob. I remember doing man's work with them but I also really remember playing like a child with them, especially Duke. Some days in the summer the animals would be in the far pasture, so I would walk out to get the milk cows and the work horses would come up to the barn with them. Normally this was just a process of getting the cows up and on their feet and headed toward the barn. Habit plus a painfully full udder usually helped accomplish this routine.

However on one memorable occasion Cowboy Larry decided he would ride Duke home, trailing his herd like any good cattleman. So I brought Duke's bridle with me this time. I caught Duke, put the bridle on him, and led him over to a fence post. Again, being a border-line genius, I positioned Duke next to the post. Then I tried climbing the post by using the barbed wire as a ladder. I will not bore you or embarrass me with the number of things that could and did go wrong with this operation. Brilliant! But after several failed attempts I finally managed to get on Duke's back. OK, remember how wide Laddie's back was? Well Duke's was almost as wide. Imagine if you will a young, short lad trying to spread his legs over that span. I might as well have tried to straddle the hood of a car, for Duke's back was about that wide and that slippery.

So, now I am spread-eagled over the horse's back, and I make my second mistake and make the 'giddy up' click with my mouth. Every step created a wonderful bounce that ended up spreading me farther, stretching my leg muscles and threatening the destruction of my 'male parts'. Again, I swear there is horse humor, because all on his own Duke decided to trot. And when a work horse trots it is neither a pretty sight…nor a comfortable one, because they barely bend their knees or ankles.

To re-create this experience I think a man would have to strip naked, and slide down a banister directly into a large oak newel post. Luckily the damage was only temporary…Jeff and Mike being the ultimate proof that they can grow back.

Chapter 4

Answering 'The Call'

I am not unique in having religion play a role in my life story, and thus having religion affect my outlook on life. I have no new information concerning theology, and no really new revelations about the impact of religion on the development of the child. My sister grew up with the same genetic and environmental background, yet I know her stories would be different than mine. This is simply the story of my remembrances of how religion impacted my life, and thus my memories of that time in my life.

I was Catholic.

I was Irish.

I was Mary Elizabeth's son.

It was the inter-play of those forces that formed the framework of my religious development. Mary Elizabeth was the daughter of Thomas Anthony Dean and Bridget Anne Lalley. Old Tom ran a good farm and got involved in local politics. My memories of Bridget or "Beezie" to the family was that she was born old, died early in my life, and combined easy love with strict religious practice. As was very usual, Tom Sr. ran the farm while Beezie cared for the house and raised their three children. The children were Katherine (Kate Brinkman), Thomas Junior, and Mom.

I know for sure Bridget tried to raise all her children the same, giving them all her shelter, her sustenance, and her religious fervor. God from Heaven called to Kate, Tom, and Mom through the true and everlasting church of St. Patrick's, of Erin Prairie, and by the mouth and prayers of Bridget Dean.

God called. Tom and Kate just didn't answer the calls. Mary Elizabeth must have heard and answered not only her calls, but the missed calls of Kate and Tom. That is my only answer for how Mom turned out, as opposed to her brother and sister. Tom and Kate were not 'hell bound spawn of Satan'. In fact religion was important to them. But they also loved to gamble, tell dirty stories, and have a wee sip…or maybe eight at times.

I remember my aunt and uncle would stop at the farm to visit. They would 'bring a bottle' because they knew we had none. Mom always kept some Canada Dry ginger ale in the basement in case someone got sick, but now it became mix!

Tom and Kate would tell stories…totally full of lies and exaggerations about some gambling they had done, and then tell some of the dirty stories they had heard. Everyone would laugh, including Mom; however, she was laughing because everyone was having a good time. Not because she approved of 'off-color' behavior.

I begin my story with these tales because Mom was deeply, devotedly, and fundamentally Catholic. But know that our home was not a theocracy run by a crazed fanatic who would rob my life of any fun or freedom.

So let's take a religious journey through my memory, and it is the reader's penance that I will not follow logic or chronology but write as the memories strike me. Like I said so often, "Hey, it's my book!"

I found some of Mom's hand written notes in the Bible she gave my wife and me for an anniversary present. Actually it was for our third anniversary. I am sure Mom was waiting to see if the marriage would last before investing in a perfectly good Bible. After all this was a mixed marriage! Mania, my wife, was of Polish and German ancestry, and while a Roman Catholic, she was not from St. Patrick's.

With typical parochial pride Mom had noted that I was the first baby to have been baptized in the newly built St. Patrick's Church. (At least two other churches had burnt before this time.) Mom noted that Patrick Cody was the first baby baptized in the newly dedicated church, but

———

Larry Moore was the first 'parishioner' to be baptized. Damn outsiders!

This new St. Pat's was a lovely church, way nicer than most of the homes in the area. But we were constantly reminded that the previous church that had been built, then burnt to the ground was almost a cathedral. These Irish Catholics knew how to build a church. Or more specifically, donate enough money to have someone build it correctly. The most impressive thing about this church was the number and size of the stained glass windows. My minds eye counts 17 windows, beautiful stained glass windows that each created a picture of some of the great events in the story of Christianity; or at least the Irish Catholic version of Christianity. The first and most prominent window on the right hand side, next to where the priest entered depicted St. Patrick dressed as a modern bishop, complete with miter and staff. There staring for eternity was Patrick, with one hand giving us the blessing and the other holding a shamrock. Standing by the waters edge Patrick's sandaled foot was crushing the last of the snakes he drove out of Ireland. (Personally, I always thought Patrick would be a saint forever if he had left the snakes alone, and kept the British out of Ireland.)

St. Patrick was on the east wall, directly across from the portals to heaven or hell. More correctly, across from Patrick was the confessional. The confessional seemed to be flat against the wall, but actually the building now increased by five feet in width on the outside of the building, allowing for a three stall confessional. The middle stall was where the priest sat, performing the Sacrament of Penance. He would sit behind a closed door, facing east. When he was ready to 'hear confession' he would pull a chain and a light above his door would be lit. He was now open for business, literally two at a time. One supplicant would enter to his right (south) through a thick purple curtain, while a second penitent would enter the left (north) room.

Confession! Confession was scheduled so many minutes before every Sunday mass or at very special times, like First Friday (the first Friday of every month). Friday night was a good confession night because a devout member of the parish could get to confession early enough to then head to Erin Corner's or McCabe's to party all night. Those wanting to rid their souls of all kinds of mortal and venial sins would line up single file on the west wall of the church.

Lining up along the wall, but, just not too close to the confessional so you couldn't hear the sins of your neighbors! But more importantly you had to set a distance and make it the 'customary' distance so no one could hear YOU!

Stand in line...Mom first, and I honestly, even to this day, have no idea what sins she could confess! Then would be my sister, next me, and finally Dad. Now I think Dad could have used a whole Friday and two priests just for himself, but that is the opinion of an abused child. If Dad and Irv were in the same line you would need an additional bishop at least.

Now Mary Elizabeth's son is standing in line, preparing to meet with God's agent on earth. I must bare my soul to this man. So I practice, "Bless me Father, for I have sinned…" But now I faced a mental and spiritual quandary. According to the laws of God, the priest, and Mary Elizabeth… what were my sins? I mentally examined the Ten Commandments and was fairly sure I had not broken any of those. Well, not broken…maybe bent, cracked or chipped a couple…but definitely not broken! So no mortal sins! Whew! That was good, because with mortal sins the priest had the right to pull a level and you fell directly through the confessional and down to hell. See, I told you Dad needed his own bishop! So let's debate venial sins. Talmudic scholars and the College of Cardinals would struggle with my attempt to list my venial sins…and were they really different from those tolerated 'little white lies' or even those outrageous lies that Dad and Irv told…those lies that were so obviously lies that no one believed them…so were they really lies?

Lies! Dad was supposed to meet Mom at a certain time when they were shopping in Baldwin. He was late; he was always late. So he would tell Mom that he had slipped off to Downing to visit an old girl friend, and they had gone dancing…was that really a lie, because even Mom was laughing. "Thou shall not steal" was confusing because shopping at Lokken Brother's in Baldwin I had seen Dad take a potato out of the bin, then he would go talk to a neighbor (and second cousin) Helen Gherrity. While talking to her he would try to slip this 'stolen' potato into her coat pocket. I remember one time he did this, and poor Helen was half way through the check out when Dad started asking in a loud voice, "Helen! Aren't you going to pay for that potato in your pocket?"

My problem as I leaned against the walls of St. Patrick's was: If everyone, including Helen laughed and thought this was a great prank by a known idiot, was it still a violation of the Seventh Commandment?   See, the problem was that there was an unstated ratio at work here: so many venial sins could add up to being a mortal sin. This was kind of an Irish Catholic "three strikes" death sentence.

So now the fateful moment, and it is my turn to enter into God's cube. I would enter, kneel on the kneeler, and wait for the priest. Suddenly a little sliding door would open. A grid of wooden slats and open spaces, covered by a sheer white veil was all that separated me from "The Man of

God!" From my very 'first confession' it hit me...I could see and identify him, so I knew he could see and identify me!

I had to tell him all my sins.

I knew him, and he knew me!

He had been in this parish forever, and he would occasionally visit our house. Now I had to tell him my innermost sins and privations! How could he not curse me in public, the vile sinner that I was, and how could I face him in public let alone in the presence of my family?

So my confession was like shopping at the local candy store: I will take ten of these 'disrespecting my parents', five of those impure thoughts, and let's make it an even dozen of those 'bad words'. Oh the agony...would God send 'the call' down to the priest to forgive me? Was I doomed to burn for ever in the fiery pit of hell or would I have to serve a yet-to-be-determined number of years getting burnt clean in purgatory?

Holding my breathe I heard, "...three Our Father's and three Hail Mary's..."

Yes! I live another day!

Sunday was the Lord's Day. Specifically that meant that you were allowed to do all your normal farm chores AND attend church service.

That 'day of rest part' pretty much lasted from 11:30 until 4:30, but a full five hours off was a really neat event.

I do not know about the rest of the world's religious people, but cattle and Catholics were predictable. You had early mass (8:00), and you had late mass (10:00) on Sunday. No matter what time the mass, some of the cattle...excuse me I meant ...... parishioners arrived late! Ten minutes into the service and the door would open and in would enter...well; you just knew who it was! You didn't have to look; it was always the Johnson family! See I picked a good non-Irish name to be sure not to offend anyone from the parish. If the 10:00 Mass was moved to 10:30 the Johnsons would still be 10 minutes late. To me, the funniest thing was these people would look at other people with an expression like, "This is the first time we have been late, and it was a crisis, and...." No one but them would believe it wouldn't happen every Sunday!

As a child I remember walking up those many steps to get to the great double doors of St. Patrick's. I remember going to mass one day, and right at the church doors Mom froze like she had looked back at Gomorrah! She had forgotten to wear a hat. No daughter of Bridget Lalley Dean would enter St. Patrick's without having her head covered! I was sent on a panic run down those steps, across State Highway G, into the parking lot to search the 1953 Mercury for anything to cover Mom's head. All I could find was an old Kleenex in the glove compartment, but Mom put it on with 'bobby pins' and entered the church like Cleopatra conquering Rome. I am sure every woman in that building could relate, and there was not a hint of embarrassment on Mom's part.

I had my personal missal so I could fully participate in the mass. Four cloth strings…red, green, blue, yellow…separated the parts of the mass, and the specific epistles and gospels for that day. That missal was the 'Reader's Digest' of Catholicism. It contained the mass, the various gospels, and the rituals of the church, the garments of the priests, and when it would rain in Calcutta! Ok, the last part is a little exaggeration, but most of what a boy needed to know about the Catholic Church was between those covers.

St. Patrick's and Mom offered a quality, in-depth education in being Catholic. Every Saturday morning during the school year, and during a two-week session during the summer, religion was taught. This religious education was directly out of The Baltimore Catechism, and it was monitored and directed by the Carmelite nuns who traveled from New Richmond to educate and save our souls. Many Catholics will tell awful stories of 'ruler wielding' nuns who terrorized their lives. Not me.

I remember Sister Vincent. I seriously think this is the first girl I ever had 'a crush on' but it has taken 50 years to admit this. A crush on a nun would violate probably eleven of Ten Commandments. God forbid I would have to confess this, and the priest would answer the call from God to send me straight to hell. To this day I remember a mass of black cloth with an edging of white…and the sweetest face this side of the Madonna. What sealed my love was that during 'recess' we would play softball, and Sister Vincent would play right along with us. It is so clear in my mind watching her reach way down between her legs; grab the bottom of her habit and pull it through her legs. She would then tuck it into the sash she wore, complete with Rosary Beads and large crucifix. I was a little boy watching a nun pull up her dress. My God, do I have to confess this? My minds eye can still see those traditional modest lace-up high heeled shoes, nylons, and skirt…all in religious black as she would belt out at least a double, and sprint around the bases like an angelic Willie Mays.

Between my crush on Sister Vincent and having Mary Elizabeth as a Mother I just wanted to be the best religious student at St. Patrick's. Sister would give an assignment of some prayer or vestment or commandment to learn. When I got home, a retired teacher and an all-time all-ways Irish Catholic Mother greeted me. She greeted me always with a hug, a kiss, and some treat…and the question, "What is today's assignment?"

So with these two wonderful and powerful women in my life of course I learned the Bible, and the vestments, and the prayers. I was way ahead of all the other students. Sister Vincent thought I had the makings of a priest. At this point all the people who have know me most of my life may commence sarcasm and laughter!

I might have to be a priest! Irish tradition was that good families often repaid the Lord by offering one of their sons to the priesthood. Ireland had more priests than rocks at one time. The world was full of Irish priests in search of a parish and souls to save. St. Patrick's church hall (read basement) had portraits of all their priests, and all of the early priests were directly from The Auld Sod.

I loved my Mom. I had a crush on Sister Vincent. I had a deep and abiding faith and love for Irish, Catholic, and St. Patrick's. And I spent many years dreading the thought that I might have to be a priest!

You have to understand, you did not chose to become a priest. Oh no! You had no choice in the matter, if you got 'The Call' you had to go! It was crystal clear that God made 'The Call' and good people answered, and without question. Noah got 'The Call' and built a boat. Jonah tried to ignore "The Call" and did penance inside the whale. Abraham got 'The Call' and almost sacrificed his only son. As a personal note, I felt some justice was served because while

Abraham probably scared the shit out of Isaac, old Abe did have to circumcise himself.

Many a night I remember Mom monitoring my bedtime. Hit the Holy Water on the window sill, then down on the knees (lovingly known as 'pray handles') for final prayers, and a good night kiss. Then I would lay there wondering if tonight was the night I would get 'The Call' and have to be a priest. Over the bed was a portrait of Christ; with a crown of thorns, holding his own heart with a dagger stabbed through it! How could I not answer 'The Call' if Jesus Christ Son of God had once answered His call from God?

Larry Moore, son of Mary Elizabeth, grandson of Bridget Lally could become a priest. But some of that damn Moore side had slipped in, and I just honestly felt I was too much of a potential sinner to be a priest. And I may add, a potential I was yearning to fulfill.

Friends and classmates were becoming altar boys, and later a cousin and classmate did 'off to the seminary'. I wouldn't even become an altar boy. I could not be an altar boy because I had farm work to do. Lie! Everyone was a farm boy! I could not understand and pronounce Latin! Well, really who could and who would know? Damn, I was caught in a cycle of 'little white lies' that was escalating into venial sins! Shit, could I deny my way into a compound mortal sin, and go to hell just because I didn't want to be a priest?

If God just didn't call for a few more years, I might be too old.

While I was hoping not to get "The Call" from Heaven, our earthly parish had its earthly business to perform. A church is an expensive operation. Money had to be raised.

As a child I had a child's set of weekly envelopes with which I could donate to Holy Mother Church. I had little envelopes that were in a box, ordered by date. I must pick the current date, put in some of my savings (nickels and dimes), and enter my name on the front. On Sunday when the collection basket was passed, I too could contribute to the welfare of St. Patrick's, and even the missions in the Belgian Congo.

Money was always an issue for 'the church'. Mom and Dad, my sister, and I would all donate what money we could. But you could also donate your 'time, talent, or treasure' to the church. We had little treasure, and God gave us little talent, but we did have some time we could give the church. On a regular bases Mom would take home the priest's vestments to be laundered. Can you imagine the religious fervor of washing and ironing the garments the priest used to perform the holy mass! Our church altar was six feet wide, so the altar cloth would be six feet plus an over-hang of two feet on either side. Now we are going to wash, hang to dry, and iron a piece of religious cloth that is three feet wide and ten feet long. I remember my sister on one end, me on the other as Mom ironed the altar cloth. Our job was to make sure not one thread of that cloth touched the floor as Mom ironed it flat and stiff. Folding an altar cloth is akin to folding the American flag. The only difference is that if you drag the American flag you don't fry in purgatory for two lifetimes.

Raising money! The Moore's actually attended two Irish Catholic churches. One was the often mentioned St. Patrick's, but the other was Holy Rosary near Cylon. One of the most unique and imaginative money raisers was the charging of 'pew rent'. Parishioners would pay for a spot in a pew where they and their family could sit. The pew spots were numbered, so you could buy one, two or how many you needed and could afford. You paid a pew rent calculated to reflect on how near the altar, and how near the pulpit you would sit. After years and even generations of this practice, the life-long members of each parish pretty much sat in the same pew every Sunday, strictly out of habit. Just like old cows to the same stanchion, we would all sit in our correct seats. On any given Sunday a blind man could 'take roll' if he too were a lifetime member.

Just like well trained cattle we all headed for the correct spot…and Oh My God…there is someone already there! The standing and milling would begin. Some would try to get into the pew anyway, with at least 10 people packed in the same small pew. Others would sit directly behind the offenders, kneel down, and basically push the offenders with their elbows. I have seen a few times where the offenders were firmly but politely informed that obviously a mistake had been made, and a re-seating needed to take place.

Every fall we would have our Annual St. Patrick's Fall Bazaar. See, that sentence is not redundant. It needed to be clear that every year we had an annual event, and the Fall Bazaar was annually held in the fall…annually!

This all made sense in Erin.

And now it was the women who got 'the call'. There was only one "The Call" but there could be many and varied 'the call' situations. Every woman in the parish was assigned a 'band' and on a rotating basis that 'band' preformed various functions for the church. A 'band' might be assigned to clean the whole church one month. Next month that 'band' would be in charge of a Sunday brunch, or serving a meal after a funeral. At this Annual Fall Bazaar, all the individual 'bands' came together to form a tribe. No, just checking to see if you really were reading. But all the bands did work at an assigned task; supplying various foods, serving the meal and waiting tables, cleaning up and washing dishes, or running any of the various games.

The men would be in charge of the cemetery, and all of that work was voluntary also. Men would be called on a regular basis for 'work detail' that would involve mowing the cemetery, straightening head-stones, and trying desperately to keep the cemetery level. Grave digging was done by the men. If someone died, 'the call' would go out and men would show up to dig the grave. Of course you brought your own shovel, but if it was winter and the ground was frozen you brought whatever you could, because that body was going to be buried! Men brought picks; they brought wood, kerosene, and even old tires to burn so they could melt the frost out of the ground. They would hit the frozen ground with picks and chisels, build a fire, and head for Erin Corners to warm up. They were very careful to warm up externally and internally. The old wood stove took care of the external, and a steady supply of beer, whiskey, and brandy warmed the innards. This was no party! This was church work!

Some times the conditions were so harsh that a bottle or two had to be brought back to the cemetery, just for severe cases of hypothermia. Plus they could toast the deceased, because death was real and death was common to these people. Death was the "Final Call" and eventually everyone had to answer that call. With all the deaths Dad faced in just his immediate family, death was just a reality to him. When you got 'the call' you went. It was as simple as that. Dad was not deep or philosophical, and he saw very little 'theology' in the whole thing. I remember nothing about him trying to make sense of why so many in his family died, and he seemed to hold no anger or bitterness. Yes, he did speak once of not being able to go on when his Mother died, but for the rest of his life she was a wonderful memory, full of love and laughter.

Dad never seemed to spend a second thinking, worrying or planning about dying. A summer storm could be raging outside…wagons tipping, barn doors slamming, and our house rocking… and Dad would be sound asleep in his rocking chair. He was asleep, he wasn't faking it. And it wasn't an attempt to show his courage or to defy God. If it was 'his time' and God sent 'the call' he would go. But if not, he was not going to waste any nap time on a thunder storm. He really believed that "…if you're born to hang, you'll never drown…" and just never cluttered his mind with worry.

Mom was always ready to die. No she was not depressed, nor more importantly depressing! She did not live her life to instill fear and dread in her family. She was just so openly and honestly prepared to answer 'the call' and go to Heaven that it was a part of her personality. As an adult I would give her a kiss, say I loved her, and say I would see her next week. And with a very content and loving smile she would say, "God willing!"

In other words, she could be dead by then. Not ever did I get the feeling she even thought that I might not be alive. No, it was God might 'call' her during that time.

Dad might be sleeping when 'the call' came, so he might miss the first few calls. Mom would want 'caller id' so she could hang up on someone to answer God's call. She was always ready. Weekly confession. Nightly rosary. Family rosary every night in Lent. Sunday mass, First Friday mass, and during Lent, Holy Thursday, and Good Friday! Mary Elizabeth, daughter of Bridget was always ready.

Hanging on the wall of Old Tom and Bridget's home, and hanging on the wall of every Irish Catholic home was an object I knew as the Mass Crucifix. Not a cross, no, first a lesson from Sister Vincent. A cross is two pieces of something that intersect. A Crucifix was a 'cross' with the body of Jesus the Christ on it!

So hanging in every home was a cross shaped box, with a Crucifix slid over the top. You would slide the Crucifix off the cross, and then set the Crucifix in a special notch in the cross box. Inside the box were also two little candles that could be stuck in holes in the crossbeams of the cross. So in a matter of seconds, the Mass Crucifix could come off the wall and be assembled into an in-house altar.

If you gave the priest 'the call' that someone in the house was injured, ill or even dying, he could drive to your house and have an instant altar on which he could perform his services. As a youth I remember practicing this ritual. It was important because 'Beezie' was always ill. Later, as Mary Irv and others aged, we could greet the priest properly, and he could see to the spiritual needs of his flock.

When electricity hit Emerald and Erin Prairie you could listen to the radio to hear the death reports. You could call the priest to come quickly to the home or the hospital. When Dad was a child the big dinner bell hanging from the windmill not only called the men from the fields, but it called the whole community to inform them of another death in his family. The means of communication could change, but the message never did.

As a young boy I found that old dinner bell out behind the workshop, buried under old metal scrap and covered with weeds and grass. Dad had no interest in the 'historical' value of this 1886 cast bell, and he didn't enjoy listening to me ring it once I had found it and cleaned it up. He had heard it ring all too often. He simply said he didn't like it because when the ladies would ring it for dinner, the horses would simply stop working no matter where they were. That made sense though it wasn't the real reason. The real reason was because of the all deaths that the bell had been used to announce.

In the Ernest Hemingway novel, "For Whom the Bell Tolls". The title comes from an old poem dealing with the belief that none of us are an island, and the death of one affects and diminishes us all. So when the bell rings announcing another death, do not ask, "…for whom the bell tolls…" because the answer is, "…it tolls for thee." And dad had heard it toll too often.

Chapter 5

Fork on the Right, Bread on the Left?

I have often been asked if I ate a lot of Irish foods when I was growing up. My answer was always, "No."

It isn't often that you get a one-word answer from an Irishman, so I will now try to do penance for that brevity by using a good number of words to try to explain what we did eat.

We ate 'farm food'.

See, I've upped it to a four-word response. Seriously, that is as true an answer as I can give. I am not an expert on foods, cooking, and the dietary habits of ethic groups in America. What I will give you may not be 'facts' but they are my memories and my opinions.

I think the one true fact throughout history is that people eat what they can in order to stay alive. What they eat, and how they prepare it is almost always the product of what they have at hand. We all think we know the 'fact' that Japanese eat raw fish. Well that is only partially true. What is true is that Japan has little arable land, wood is a precious commodity, and most Japanese live relatively close to the sea.

So did my family eat traditional Irish foods? What I remember is that we ate 'farm foods' like everyone else in our neighborhood. Many people are aware that the Irish eat potatoes. Many people know about the famous potato famines in Ireland. All this is true. In the 1840's Ireland consumed more potatoes than any nation in Europe. As the Irish population was forced off 'the land' by the British, and as what little land they did own for themselves was both full of rocks and full of kids, growing a food crop like potatoes was about all they could do.

To me, some things are so simple. Why do you think the guards at the Tower of London were nicknamed 'beef eaters'? Because the reward for this prestigious job was a large allotment of beef! The aristocracy of Europe 'ate high on the hog' because they got the best, most preferred part of the pig, while those at the bottom got 'nothing but the squeal'. What Scotsman if given free choice of any part of the sheep would say, "Of course I want the stomach Lad! And stuff it full of wheat and berries too! "Aye, who'd eat lamb chops when there's cold haggis to be had?"

The Irish or more specifically the 'landed gentry' that were my ancestors ate potatoes. And when the blight hit, they starved. Close to one-third of the Irish population died. Those that could, emigrated, somewhere… anywhere!

Those that made it to America did not come with wonderful ethnic recipes in mind. Traditional Irish food would probably be 'black-blighted potato'. In maybe a distant memory there might be a romantic tale of 'corned beef and cabbage' or even 'mulligan stew' but those would be very rare.

My first experience with corned beef was at a St. Patrick's Day celebration in the basement of St. Patrick's Church. Strictly my opinion, but I think that was a typical and universal example of people trying to get back in touch with "the Irish in 'em' just like putting green dye in pancakes, cookies, and beer. I honest to God can not fathom green beer! Saints preserve us!

Did we eat Irish food on St. Patrick's Day? Only if St. Patrick's Day fell on a Sunday, then we might go straight to the parish basement after mass and 'be Irish' for a while.

Any other St. Paddy's Day was a work day, and we came to the house to eat good plain food.

And just as an aside: If you remove vegetables from the list, just how many 'green' foods would you want to eat? If it was March 16th or 18th and someone gave you a green slice of bread, would you eat it? How about green cheese? My German neighbors, who would eat raw hamburger, certainly would not eat green raw hamburger.

As I repeat so often, my family ate 'farm food'. Did we eat a lot of potatoes? Yes, but our German neighbors ate a lot of potatoes. And so did our Norwegian and Polish neighbors. The fact was you could grow your own potatoes or buy a 'gunny sack' full at a very reasonable price. We Moores ate potatoes, but everyone else ate potatoes too.

The biggest bowl on the 'thrashing table' was full of boiled potatoes, and it didn't matter if this was an Irish house or Polish house or a German house. We all ate lots of potatoes, prepared in many different ways. Left-over boiled potatoes could be sliced into fried potatoes. Fill the cook stove with raw potatoes and come back later to baked potatoes: eat the inside, and re-bake the outside for potato skins filled with lots of butter. We all ate potatoes, but what I remember most is that there were good cooks, and there bad cooks…not ethnic cooks.

Mom was a good cook. And she made 'farm food'. If she had a recipe book it probably had 3 pages. She did have a recipe box with little reminders written neatly on scraps of paper. Later they would be re-written on the famous 3 x 5 cards every good cook must have…and exchange with other good cooks. I wish I knew just how many 'ethnic recipes' were lost as old time cooks aged and their 'cook from memory' creations were not able to be replicated by the next generation. Some could not write, but I think some just wanted to 'guard' their creations and bask in the knowledge that 'no one could make bread like grandma'.

As a good cook, mom had two simple guidelines: quality, then quantity. Whether she was cooking for our little family, special guests, or a horde of thrashers, Mom prided herself on making a good meal, with lots to eat. I think it is an ingrained, almost genetic trait in people that the quality of food and the volume of it will signal your status in this world. We may have been 'poor' (always a debatable term) but we ate well. We may have been poor but no guest or thrasher left the Moore table hungry, and you hoped they also were impressed.

My bet is that anyone reading this story, regardless of ethnic background, can tell stories of their ancestors preparing more food than you could ever eat at two sittings! You will remember, especially 'the woman of the house,' encouraging everyone to "…oh, have just a bit more!" Can you remember your "ethnic grandma" not eating her pie, but sliding her piece over to you just after you barely got your own piece eaten? And how many 'left-over's' did you have to take home when you left? Can you hear, "Please take some home, we will just have to throw it out!" And of course you did NOT throw it out, but you ate left-over's for days. Nothing got thrown out!

Any meal eaten at Mary Elizabeth's house consisted of three parts. The first part was the preparation, the second part was the eating, and the third part was the clean up. No one part was more important than the other, and no part could be eliminated or rushed.

Preparation took as long as it took! If this meant starting days ahead, then you started days ahead. Bread would be cut into cubes, dried on top of the tall 'china closet', and then finally baked in the oven to make stuffing. This might take a week. Bread dough would be prepared in the morning, put in pans and covered with damp towels, then put up on the china closet to rise at its own pace in the warmest part of the house. Potatoes in that big Wear Ever cooker would boil just a little longer than required because there will NOT be any raw places in Mom's potatoes, and it was almost a sin if there were lumps in either the mashed potatoes or gravy.

Meat took as long as it took! There were no parasites or other questionable things in mom's meat because everything was cooked just a touch past well done, yet you could cut it with your fork. Chicken must fall off the bone. We were aware that Jews did not eat pork, and we did know what our pigs ate, so Mom made cooking pork a religious experience...she cooked the hell out of it!

The second part of the meal was the eating. Dad would come into the house, and no mater what, Dad would wash his hands, his face, and comb his hair before sitting at the table. This was not Irish, this was good manners. I remember the thrashers would always do this also. They would all 'clean up' before a meal. At some farms they would use the pump jack; at some ladies would provide a wash stand and bowl under a tree; while at other houses it was just a couple of buckets of water set on the lawn.

Taking turns someone would pump the handle or pour from the pail while others washed. Several would get their hands wet at the same time, passing the one bar of soap around. More water to rinse with, and then often sharing the same towel at the same time. This was 'thrasher style' and even as a child I knew this was more ritual and manners than real cleanliness, because in my minds eye I can still see that the bar of soap was no longer white and that one towel was no longer spotless when the men were done 'washing'.

My memories of most meals center on the food, and the conversations. The food part should be obvious, the conversation part is also very important. No matter where we ate, there seemed to be constant conversation. I honestly think those 'communal' thrashing meals made the whole dirty harvesting operation something the men looked forward to every year. .

Even at the crowded 'thrasher table' I was allowed to sit with the men. We had no 'big people – little people' tables. And I was allowed to talk…and was given a respectful hearing. There was no sense that one person's opinion was more important than another's.

At home we all had 'assigned' seats, but this was mainly because Mom wanted to sit to the south. This put her in easy reach of the refrigerator, the stove, and the sink. The bonus to this was that because our old house was starting to sag, sitting to the south put Mom on the 'low side' of the table. Anything spilled would always run Mom's way, and Mom always wore an apron!

Mom served the food, and the plates were full. Now it was time to say the before-meal grace. The ritual was so ingrained that Dad knew immediately when he could pre-empt Mom's prayers with something like, "Hail Mary full of grace, wipe the potatoes off my face." Just as routine were Mom's reprimands of Dad and the very real possibility of him going to hell. Unlike some Christian's, Mom never bowed her head nor closed her eyes when she prayed. I am now convinced this had less to do with religious conviction and more to do with keeping a watchful eye on her three children…Margie, me and Dad, Dad being the worst!

Once the 'real grace' had been said, the meal could begin. Eating and talking dominated. There was really very little reaching or asking for something. The table was small and the few 'condiments' would be in the center of the table. If you used something…return it to whence it came! Salt did dominate our table, and control of the salt shaker would be akin to the modern situation of dominating the remote control for the TV! You just did not use the salt, and leave it at the edge of your plate. Bad manners! If you did you would hear, "Church in the middle of the parish!" Like the extra glass of wine for Isaiah, pepper was on the table in case Irv ate with us.

And of course there was always butter in the center.

The butter is important because at our table there were four eating utensils: knife, fork, spoon, and bread. Bread may be the historical 'staff of life' but it was more than a food in our house. Bread was a food AND a tool. You used your 'bread tool' to aid in eating other foods. With your 'metal tool' in one hand and your 'bread tool' in the other you could move peas and corn onto your fork; you could move potatoes and gravy over to the meat, which you had cut with your fork. The 'bread plate' was also near the middle of the table where Mom would place over a half a loaf of pre-sliced homemade bread. A thick slice slathered with butter and folded in half made a great tool…and you didn't have to wash it when you were done!

And the last bit of bread could be used to wipe the plate clean; making sure you 'cleaned your plate before dessert'.

Timing and proportion were learned over time; because it would be a quandary that would stump even Solomon if you finished your bread but still had food left on your plate. What to do? Do I leave that last few bites or do I butter another whole slice of bread? And unlike Solomon, the solution was not to cut it in half.

Most meals must end in dessert. Now if you are thinking, that is dumb because who eats dessert after a breakfast of Fruit Loops? Remember, pre-processed breakfast meals arrived late in farm history. A nice piece of pie or cake after breakfast was not at all unusual. So a great meal must end with a great dessert. A meal without a dessert would be "…like a kiss without a hug!"

The after-meal grace marked the end of the eating part of the meal.

Now the third part of the meal would take place. The whole kitchen would be made 'neat-and-clean' again. Neat and clean were not separate concepts to Mom. A house could not be neat if it was not clean, and it could not be clean if it was not neat. Mom could separate salt from pepper; she could understand to without fro; she could even grow to accept Irish without Catholic. But she could never separate 'neat-and-clean'.

This was NOT Irish or Catholic. This was Mom, and Bridget Lally Dean pure and simple. We had neighbors who were both Irish and Catholic and their kitchen's looked like Rome after the Huns were done raping and pillaging. This was not ethnic, it was learned.

The table was not only emptied, it was washed. Any and all equipment used in preparing or eating the meal must be washed. Everything was washed, rinsed, then hand-dried, and put back in its proper place. Mom's counter tops had basically nothing on it for two good reasons: it would all have to be moved during each clean up, and when you only had about four feet of counter-top you didn't waste it with cute little containers. And besides, flour came in a 25 pound bag, and was stored in its own huge flour bin. Sugar came in 10 pound bags, and the bag was often in the flour bin.

By the time I entered high school my sister had found a job and had moved away. Mom decided she would get a job to bring in some much needed cash. So in summer, Dad and I were home alone most of the day. Mom would prepare a basic meal the night before, but I had to finish getting the noon meal ready. Our meals were simple so I acquired no great culinary skills, but did gain the attitude that there were not 'male jobs' and 'woman's work' in our family.

If Mary was sick Irv would join us, but it was usually Dad and me. When the eating was done, Dad would adjourn to the living room to read the paper or farm journal. Since Dad had quit school after 4th grade he was really not much of a reader, so this was just an excuse to take a nap. I had clean up duty on my own, and it was understood by all that Mom would never come home to a messy kitchen.

Dad would be snoring in his favorite rocking chair, and I would be 'neating and cleaning' as quiet as possible. Now I would love to tell you this was because I was just that saintly a child, but the truth is that I was hoping I could finish the dishes and sneak past Dad for a little quality sofa time of my own.

No luck. No luck ever. I would barely reach the sofa and Dad would be wide awake. Maybe Dad just had a great internal clock, but I was always suspicious that God would send Dad 'the call' to wake up, just to punish me for refusing to be a priest.

Remember, the Old Testament God was an angry God who would not fail to exact his punishments. Vengeance is Mine Sayith the Lord.

Did we eat Irish? No, but we did eat Catholic. One of the dominating factors for all Catholics through history was that every Friday and all of Lent was to be meatless. For centuries Lent meant 'fast and abstinence' for the whole period, although even among devout Catholics there were many battles over how to get 40 Days of Lent out a 46 day time span. Lent was a true test of faith for both the soul and the body. And both were taxed during this period of demands and privation. Many Catholics in 'old Ireland' were starting to break under the harsh demands of this fasting and abstaining. This denial may be acceptable if you are well fed the rest of the year, but 40 days of increased denial for an already challenged population was becoming too much for some Irish. With England already escaped or expelled from the true church (depends on your point of view) and now totally protestant, many Irish Catholics were tempted to 'fall away' themselves, and escape the severe limitations on their lives. To prevent Irish Catholics cheating during Lent or…God Forbid…turn to being Protestants, the powers in Rome lifted these harsh and severe restrictions on the Irish for one day during Lent. St. Patrick's Day! Just think…in the midst of Lent the Irish were allowed a one day Mardi Gras. The restrictions were lifted and the Irish could eat anything and as much as they wanted, and consume alcohol without restrictions. So most Irish stayed Catholic, and Patrick was truly a 'Saint'.

Eventually the rules were further changed to fasting through lent and abstinence from meat only on Fridays and Ash Wednesday. So maybe during lent you gave up candy or chocolate. I do remember sitting in church and hearing the priest clear his throat and read the letter from the Bishop in Superior. Even though it was probably the same letter every time, we at St. Pat's would be given the rare and singular privilege to have our Lenten restrictions lifted so we could have our annual St. Patrick's Day feast with corned beef, even when it fell on a Friday.

But for most of our meatless Friday's of the year Mom had to be very creative. Some meals were pancakes, Johnny cake or cornbread muffins covered with either honey or home-made syrup (one cup water, four cups sugar, one tablespoon of Watkin's mapleline). Occasionally we had fish, with red sockeye salmon being the main course. The salmon came out of a can in a round, packed mass with the spinal column still there. You could eat the bones because the processing made them so soft. But it was butter; butter slathered thickly over a slice of Mom's bread that allowed the dry salmon to make it down your throat. There was also cod to eat. It came in a 6 inch x 4 inch x 2 inch wooden box with a sliding cover. You could boil this and eat it with potatoes, but that was really too Norwegian! But those wooden boxes were cherished as a place to store special treasures.

In conclusion, if we did eat 'ethnic' it was most likely not Irish. We did not eat Irish potatoes; we ate lots of dry white russets. We ate Spanish rice, Swiss steak, French toast, English muffins,

Polish sausage, and Italian spaghetti. And even if it was for one special day, why put green dye in a great bottle of Leinekugel's or Pabst?

Speaking of drinking. In the winter months we would have to get corn and oats milled for added food for the cows. We would load the hayrack with sacks of raw grain, and have the horses pull the wagon to Emerald for milling. While the grain was being milled the three Irish men (Dad, Irv and I) would walk to Bernard Frye's bar. And though I was just a kid, I was allowed sips of my Dad's beer as I sat on his lap. There we would talk and laugh and drink with a united nations of nationalities. Just read the names: DeLong and Lettellier (French), Hurtgen and Klatt (German), Pole and Pohl (Polish, and relatives!), Stevens and Stephens (with an Irish and a German in each spelling), Knutson and Larson from Norway, along with the Kennedy's and the Moore's.

And after sharing a little bar time, each would head to their respective homes to eat 'farm food' for supper.

Chapter 6

"Mary, can you lighten that picture a little?"

My Dad was born June 2, 1902. On December 18, 1903 the Wright brothers flew an airplane 150 feet. When he was 65 years old, Dad flew to New York to visit his daughter, and the plane he flew on had a wing span that was almost the same as the length of Wright's first flight! By the time Dad died, twelve Americans had walked on the moon.

As a young man Dad and the thrashing crew would work over two weeks to get the grain harvested. The last years Dad farmed Doug Goodrich would arrive with three self-propelled combines, two gravity boxes, a grain truck, and an elevator…and he was done in two hours.

I am not sure if any generation will ever see the transformations and transitions that Dad's generation witnessed.

I live by several quotes, as mentioned before, one of the most lasting is, "It is not how old you are, but what was it like when you were young." Ours was a hard life; a life full of work and difficult situations; a life I would not want to repeat and would never wish on my sons or grandsons. And yet....and yet there is something so special about this experience that I need to steal a phrase from William Manchester who wrote "....he always viewed it through a rose colored nimbus...."

Now most of the 'heroes' of this little story would at this point say, "What the hell did he just say? And what the Jasus (Jesus pronounced Jay sus so as not to use the Lord's name) is a nimbus?"

OK, it was a tough life but it was a life full of love and laughter also. As another old line says, "If I wasn't laughing, I'd be crying." As hard or as stupid as much of it was, they approached life full force. Bad things happening was normal so why not find something to laugh about. Even though this next story is out of the time frame, I think it could have come from my Dad not Billy Hermansen.

True story. Billy goes to the hospital to visit a friend who had just gone through a whole load of bad luck, including the removal of one foot. Everyone in the room was silent, sad, depressed or in shock.

And Billy says to the guy, "Cheer up. Just think of the money you'll save on socks!"

Silence.

Followed by snickers and giggles and finally outright laughter. And the one laughing the hardest was the patient. This is just the kind of thing Dad would have loved.

As a child, Dad and his family "…went to bed with the chickens…" because once it was dark, all they had were oil lamps and candles.

But eventually, electricity arrived; lights were possible; and eventually a radio brought the outside world to Emerald. Dad and Irv used to spend some Friday nights together listening to boxing matches on the radio. Both Dad and Irv were big fans of that great Irish champion Archie Moore, and it was always a special Friday night when Archie would be the feature on "The Gillette Cavalcade of Sports" or simply the 'fight night' to most people.

When I was about 10 years old we transitioned into the television age. Some kind of motley aluminum antenna was strapped to the chimney and a flat brown 'ribbon wire' ran from the antenna down the side of the house and in through a window in the living room, and was attached to the television… which was about half the size of a refrigerator. I do not remember the day of the week we got it, but soon Friday arrived and now through the miracle of modern science the Moore's could watch "Irish Archie" boxing, live, in person, with our own eyes!

Can you feel the drama building? "…in the white trunks…weighing in at 186 pounds… Archie… Moore………What…..?

Archie Moore was an African-American!

I still remember…silence!

Followed by snickers and giggles.

Not one swear word. Not one racist remark.

Dad turns to Mom and says, "Mary can you lighten that picture a little?"

Ah television! A huge box, that seemed to go through tubes every month. At first programming did not start until about 10:00 a.m. on weekdays, and went off-air after the 10:00 p.m. news. The rest of the time all you got was the famous 'test pattern'. Weekend programming started earlier and ran later…usually until midnight, and ended with the American Flag waving and the playing of the National Anthem.

Most of the time you could get four stations: 4, 5, 9, and 11. Most of the time….unless there was a storm interfering with transmission. Or the storm might simply twist the roof antenna so the transmissions could not be picked up. So 'someone' would have to climb up on the roof. Guess who that 'someone' often was? I told you I was abused.

First you get a ladder, which of course was a home made ladder which may have been used by Noah to exit the ark. Step two was to lean the ladder against the porch roof, and climb onto the porch. Step three was to pull the ladder up behind you, and lean it against the roof valley where two gables met. Step four was to again climb the ladder, then keep climbing up the roof to the peak.

Note: We had three porches, with three valleys so you rotated which one you used because: a) this was a frequent event and b) you did not want to wear out the shingles! If the weather was really hot you did not fix the antenna until it cooled down in the evening or waited a couple of days until the weather changed. Hot weather and shingles didn't mix.

Now at best this was a three person operation: one on the roof, one on the ground, and one inside with the TV. So now the idiot on the roof twists the antenna a little, and then yells "OK" to the person on the ground. The person on the ground yells "OK" to the person watching the TV. TV watcher yells to the person on the ground, "Better" (or worse) so the person on the ground yells the same direction to the idiot on the roof. This bonding experience could go on for a long time because while "Better" might mean better for channel 4 it could also mean worse for channel 9.

One time we did this exercise for about 30 minutes, with every twist resulting in a "Worse" response. By sheer accident someone then discovered that the 'ribbon wire' had simply become unconnected. Oh did we laugh about that...NOT!

Eventually Mary and Irv also got a TV. Mary insisted she would never watch it because she had so much housework to do. But she would allow it to be on some of the time, and apparently 'some of the time' seduced her into becoming a professional wrestling addict. Of course she would never admit this, but during the summers when all the doors and windows were open you would hear her screaming; sometimes she was damming the villain and other times warning or encouraging the good guys. There was a time that I think Mary would have left Irv for Verne Gagne.

One warm summer evening our family of four were in the dining room when this blood curdling scream of "Oh My God" came from the other house. Mom said, "Wrestling must be wild tonight." Dad immediately came back with, "Or Irv is throwing her on the bed!"

It didn't take long for Mom to reach for the Rosary Beads but I doubt there was much plenary indulgence granted that evening.

Chapter 7

Potato Vines (Irish <u>Roots</u>)

Remember those two re-occurring expressions: "It's not how old you are, but what was it like when you were young", and "If you you're born to hang, you'll never drown".

I want it clear, we were poor but we were never in poverty; we struggled but we never felt privation; and life was often backwards and crude, but that was more by conscious decision rather than any whim of the Gods. No, we were not in the lap of luxury but our family fate was honestly better than so many people, both then and now.

I honestly have no idea if the way I tell a story has anything to do with being Irish. And I don't know whether our family's stories, decisions, and reactions were part of our Gaelic make-up. But 'being the Irish' is the way so many things were related to me as a youth, that despite lots of years and a little education I still fall back on 'me Irish' for answers. And if this story takes too long, and twists like a blackthorn cane, well, I am the author, not you. As I heard so often, "Make haste slowly lad, you'll be dead a long time."

I am not going back to when Moses was a pup, but with the story of Joseph Moore and his beloved Mary Brown. Joe's father had built a long cabin on a piece of rock…ooops, rather firm soil in what is Emerald Township. Joe's father was named Lawrence(my great grandfather). Once again, I never fail to be impressed with the names these creative people used. Just like the hay went in the hay mow, and the horses in the horse barn, human names were just as imaginative. If your name wasn't Lawrence, it was Joseph, and then Joseph would have a son who he would dutifully name Lawrence.

This is a true aside to the story; when I was young there were five Lawrence Moore's on our Emerald mail route. To eliminate confusion, one was called by his full name, one by his middle initial, one by his first two initials, one as Larry, and one as Lonnie.

Of course these men usually married, and when they did it was usually to a Mary. Or an Elizabeth. Some were creative enough to wed a Mary Elizabeth, but that was just showing off. My mother was scheduled to be named Elizabeth, but she was born on the Feast of the Immaculate Conception and the priest basically refused to baptize her unless she was named Mary. So Mary Elizabeth Dean was entered into the baptismal records. Getting completely off the track, my Dad married Mary Elizabeth and his brother wed Mary Katherine Murtha. Not to mention Dad and Irv had a sister Mary.

I love these convoluted stories. I can just visualize some future 'proof reader' screaming, "What the hell is going on here. Where in hell are we?" Luckily my wife is editing my book and she is used to my convoluted stories…eye roll.

Hang on. We are going to Erin Prairie for a second, where fascinating neighbors named Mae and Russell Gherity lived. Mae gave birth to five daughters, and they named them all Mary! Each of the girls grew up with the name Mary, but they were called by their middle names.

So the original Lawrence Moore was born in Ireland in 1834 or 1836. Those damn Irish are such sticklers for accuracy! Original Lawrence immigrated to America, where he meets and weds Catherine Clancy. Now maybe the name gave you a little clue, but Catherine was Irish. Any of the "Moore Records" I have seen have a question mark next to Catherine's date of birth and the site of that birth, other than it was in Ireland.

Catherine met Lawrence and was immediately smitten by his rugged good looks, his skill at music and poetry, and a significant amount of gold coin. This last sentence is completely made up, but then I have read James Michener when he describes the thoughts, passions, and decision to mate attributed to a Chesapeake Bay clam. This is either called literary license or Irish Bull Shit, I can't remember which.

Anyway, these two children of the Emerald Isle were married in Hudson, Wisconsin in the year 1860. The specifics of how they arrived in Emerald Township are unclear, but there are stories that the Catholic priest in Hudson would walk to Erin Prairie to care for the spiritual needs of the Irish in that area. I do think it is more than coincidence that the Catholic churches in both Hudson and Erin Prairie are named St. Patrick's. There is also a story that the church in Erin Prairie was actually the 'home church' for a 'mission church' in that little mill town of New Richmond.

This could turn into a saga like Alex Haley's "Roots" if I don't get back on track. So Kunta Moore...ooops, Lawrence Moore begets Joseph Moore. And after a lot of biblical-style begetting and begatting we end up with a large farm house built by Joseph, in which Mary delivered nine children. I don't know the exact acreage but Joe did accumulate a nice chunk of land. He was not only a farmer but a wheeler and dealer in cattle and especially horses. By the standards of the day he had made a very good life for himself and his family. The house was large, with at least six bedrooms upstairs. There was a parlor that was separated from the rest of the house by a set of sliding pocket doors. In modern terms, there was a picture window in the living room and people entered through a door that had leaded stained glass surrounds. The front door was approached by walking onto a covered porch that ran the length of that side of the house. The dining room was the largest room, and it could be entered by a door from the north or a door from the south. Each of those entrances was coved by a roofed porch.

I have no proof, but stories told to me as a youth by people other than my own family claimed that Joe Moore was a wealthy man by the standards of that time. From old broken down items I found over the years I found he had all kinds of horse equipment, and he used to earn money by tending to the needs of other people's horses. One strange relic I found in oat chaff that had built up over the years was a hand-cranked horse clipper for cutting and grooming horses. There were long handled rasps for filing down horses back teeth (long teeth could kill a horse), and every kind of horse shoe and piece of Ferrier equipment. There were shoes of huge work horses; shoes for horses on muddy ground; on frozen ground; shoes for ponies and colts; there were shoes to correct a limp or a spilt hoof, and even one set that appeared broken…until I was informed they were for oxen.

So what happened to the wealth, what happened to the ancestors?

They died.

There were nine children who lived for a while. The little bit of our history I have been able to put together comes from various sources, and after many years. Dad and Irv especially did not want to spend much time discussing their family's past. Healthy or not, repressed or suppressed or in denial, Dad and Irv and even Mom to some extent did not dwell on the past. Irish fatalism? "If you're born to hang…" Just plain coping with reality and moving on? I'm not sure, but death was a real part of life for these people.

Nine live births. Henry Irvin was born first in 1893! When he entered the army, they got his first and middle name mixed and he became Irv. It was Irv on not just his Army pay, but every legal document from the Army and later as he met medical challenge after medical challenge, it was used at the Veteran's Hospital. And because Henry served in the Army during WWI, upon his return our neighbor Miles Kennedy addressed him as 'the colonel'.   I think Henry just surrendered and accepted that Irvin was just easier. So the first born became Irvin Henry.

My Dad, Lawrence Edward Moore was born on June 2, 1902. He should have died. Severely under weight (about two pounds), he was soon hit with a rupture and chicken pox. He struggled, but did survive.

In 1905 his brother John died, having not survived a year.

In 1906 his brother Charles died, having not survived a year.

In 1918 his Father died in his sleep, probably a heart attack.

In 1921 his Mother died in the hospital from gall bladder complications.

In 1923 his sister Margaret died, and was buried in what was to be her wedding dress.

Henry, now called Irvin came home from military service to become head of the family. Irv married Mary and they moved into the family house, just like the Walton's or any other extended family.

Brother Joseph (of course there was a Joseph!) moved out, and got married. He received 80 acres from the farm as his inheritance. They had no money, so land was their capital. This Joe would father several children, and then be dead by 1939. Rightfully that land went to his wife and children.

Brother Celestine....wait a minute! Where in the hell did that name come from? Celestine, and they called him Stein. Modern political correctness prevents me from just going off on...oh, it is so tempting. OK, I have done some research and found a Pope with that name, possibly a Saint Pope. But you feed me a Joseph-Lawrence-Mary-Elizabeth diet, and then slip in a Stein and it just snaps my mental garters.

Anyway, Stein got another 80 acres and wed Mary Rose Meath. She was always Mary Rose, and she never aged a day until she left us. It would be a beautiful story except Stein died in May of the year I was born (1946) and they had neither kit nor kin. (I know it is kith nor kin but we Moore's said kit).

And again, that land went to Mary Rose. Small compensation for her! She remained a lovely and gracious widow for the rest of her days. Soon the 'little girls' grew up and wanted to leave. Guess what? One was named Mary, and the other was named Elizabeth! Mary and Elizabeth were family, but more importantly their gender meant nothing, and it was just a matter of fact that they too would get the same acreage. They did not want the land because their jobs, then marriages took them to the big cities in Minnesota, so they sold the land for their inheritance.

By now a rather substantial land holding had been whittled down to 240 acres. Some of the family had moved on, some had died. It was now Irv and his wife Mary, their daughters Margaret and Lorraine, and bachelor Dad living in the big old house. The once impressive house had suffered over the years from lack of money. The house also had some rough use as confirmed by this story that was often told by Dad and Irv (therefore it is almost Biblically true!) of the time when they were children. Irv opened both the south and north door to the dinning room, and Dad rode a work horse through one door, across the dining room, and out the other door. I tell you, we Moore's are natural equestrians! To me, what is really significant is not that Dad and Irv were pranksters (read little shits) but that they both insist that their Mom was there and she almost passed out from laughing so hard. I mean riding an 1800 pound horse through your dinning room…this is high comedy. No wonder when Dad could speak of his Mother, it was always about this big laughing and loving woman.

As mentioned before, he had wished he too could have died on the day he learned she was gone forever. She went to the hospital and never came home. All of his life Dad had a 'reaction' to the idea of going to the hospital. The irony is the only time he went to the hospital; he did not come home either.

By 1940, five deaths and four marriages had changed the dynamics and fortunes of the family.

Luckily the Great Depression came just in time to spice things up!

And the icing on the cake was that during the Depression one of the worst droughts in American history hit mid-America. True, Wisconsin was not in the classic Dust Bowl but the state did have a severe shortage of rain.

Millions of Americans suffered during the Great Depression. And the suffering of most Americans does not rival the suffering in most of Europe and Asia. So I am not begging for sympathy, I am just trying to put it all into a Moore perspective.

The Great Depression was one of the most impactful events in American history. It was bad, it was terrible, but it was NOT totally negative. Some of what we 'are as Americans', is because we suffered and struggled through the Great Depression, and World War II. The Great Depression was terrible! It almost destroyed our nation, our world. And yet the people who struggled, and the people who survived often view it as a seminal point in their lives. I did not battle the Great Depression so I can only view it from the outside, and filter it through the experiences of my family. History books can give us data and facts and stories, but they become real when your own flesh and blood tell you personal stories about this time period.

There is a 'survival mentality' for so many Depression Era people. To have survived the Depression and WWII had to impact what Tom Brokaw calls, "The Greatest Generation". There is a type of 'war stories' mentality here. These are people who survived the un-survivable. They almost tell martyr stories. There is a morbid sense of defeat, mixed with a sense of pride and accomplishment that I feel incapable of putting into words. It is almost like being that lone survivor of an air plane crash. This survivor may suffer from a dichotomy of feelings…a sense of guilt and confusion mixed with a sense of success and entitlement. Millions of people can tell millions of stories about these years.

Dad and Irv would tell of sending the horses to the lumber camps because they couldn't feed them. They would tell of shipping a large, fat cow to market in South St. Paul, and when the cost of processing and shipping were deducted, they owed the truck driver! A net loss on what was to be their profit margin that year. Dad told of milking his cows and doing his chores, then heading off to work for 'the government'. I don't know if it was for Emerald Township, the state of Wisconsin or the WPA, but Dad worked away from home for some desperately needed cash. He would provide himself and a team of horses for work on the local roads. He would work, then feed himself and his horses, then work some more until his ten hour shift was over. That would earn him $1.00!

So what was left of the Moore family, dug in and tried to survive, like millions of other people. Money not spent became more significant than the possibility of money gained. They were used to physical labor and denying themselves, so just play to your strength. No money was wasted on frivolous items, and any child of the Depression can make a list of what was really frivolous!

Their power and pride was in never surrendering! They surrendered a lot of things that today we would call necessities, but they gave them up. They did not spend on the house, but they never lost the land. They dried up cows rather than feed them, but they kept them alive. If you could not grow it or create it on the farm, you did not have it.

When Dad first met Mom, she was a school teacher. She taught at an Erin Prairie school, and then at a Stanton public school. And we are talking one room, eight grades, and the teacher gets to school early enough to light the fire and perform 'janitorial duties' before classes began. The hard and fast rule in 'the good old days' was that a married woman would not be allowed to continue to teach. The 'single, devoted only to education woman' was the norm at the time. Norm…that is why River Falls, and many other schools were first called 'normal schools', because they taught future teachers the 'norms' or standards the state expected in education.

Mom was engaged to Dad, and started putting money aside. When she decided to get married she should have lost her career, but she 'used the brain God gave her' and negotiated with the Stanton school board. They couldn't find a replacement right away, so she 'agreed' to teach for one year as a married woman so they could find a virgin...ooops, a single woman to meet the sanctity of educational expectations.

Sorry, but I have to vent my spleen. I was hired as a teacher in 1969, now read that again...1969! A woman teacher was hired that same year. During the school year she discovered she was pregnant. She was a married woman who had five prior children, but she was now pregnant as a teacher! Her contract was not renewed! Luckily she was able to deliver this devil child, and re-apply for her job later that fall. The school board in all there benevolence, agreed to rehire her. Hopefully she could control her reproductive urges. I mean we are talking education here! What do babies and children and education have in common!?!? That Board of Education was made up of five old men whose gonads were about the size of mustard seeds, and had not smiled since Coolidge was President. They knew what was best for American education?

So Mom knew her career was over, and she was going to be a married ex-teacher. Who could not give up a salary and a career to marry a Moore?

During the last two years of her career Mom packed away as much money as she could. Time and inflation distort everything, but she saved enough money to buy a complete dinning room set; a table with expandable leaves, eight chairs, a china closet, and a buffet. All of this cost her a grand total of $75.00 (about one year's wages) which is meaningless in today's economy but a total commitment on her part.

The rest of her savings went toward building a house. The 'deal' was that Mom and Dad would build Irv, Mary, and the girls (Margaret and Lorraine) a new house. Then Mom and Dad would inherit the old family house. I have seen the house that was built; after all it was my second home! It was a modest house, but it was new. That was a major factor because the original farm house had fallen into disrepair by this time. Mary and Irv got a new house for the kingly ransom price of $1,111.11.

I saw the original total, and that is the correct total price. You can't make that up!

Irv and Mary and girls moved into a new house. My Mother was the invading bitch! Why? Margaret and Lorraine were jealous because this new lady was stealing Lawrence away. Dad was their favorite 'brother', and the guy that made them laugh and was their second dad. I mean it was Lawrence who taught them how to do all the wonderful things like tell dirty stories, or to swear, or to chew and spit tobacco. It was the dynamics of the Moore's that for as many crude things Lawrence taught these girls, Mary Murtha

Moore blamed Irv for everything, and treated Dad-Lawrence as her cute little brother. Honest, in my whole life I had never ever heard Mary-Irv say one cross or negative thing about Lawrence.

The trade off was Dad never once said a negative thing about Irv. Irv was a combination of Brother-Father-God to Dad. I remember late in life when Irv was really slipping. The worst and only thing Dad would ever say is, "That's Irv." Irv had earned Dad's love and respect over a long time! By the time I was about ten years old, Dad and I were doing most of the work. OK, Dad was doing most of it! But Irv got half the income, what ever that was. Dad did all the milking, and Irv got half the milk check. Even Irv's grown daughter's said this was wrong, yet Dad would not bend on taking more than half. This was Irv! Don't you get it! He kept us together, and we are family. End of story.

I remember Dad and Irv doing 'end of the year' taxes, and the only fight they would have was who deserved the most income. But it was in reverse, because Dad insisted Irv deserved 'this much', but Irv would counter with NO it was Dad who really deserved the lion's share. Even now I am blown away by the sense of....well love, because it made no financial sense.

Many years later when Dad was old, and Irv was in the rest home I went to Baldwin to get Irv from the institution, and brought him to Emerald for

Thanksgiving. I brought this old man into his old home, and he walked over to where Dad was sitting, sat down, and they starting talking like they had never been apart. It was like they had just left the barn, and once again outsiders were interfering on there normal conversation.

That is the power of family love!

Now why did these two old farts go through so much? Well part was their personalities, and part were their decisions during an evolutionary part of American history.

And part was due to the power being out of their hands.

Chapter 8

The Power and the Glory

One of the most evolutionary and revolutionary aspects of American life was the introduction of electricity to the masses.

Please stand by for a quick history lesson.

Mankind had known about electricity for years. By 1880 Thomas Edison had developed a working light bulb, and by 1882 his electrical company was stringing wires and supplying electricity to customers in New York City.

By 1930 about 90% of the people in urban America were hooked up to electricity. 90% of URBAN Americans had electricity, and thus the revolutionary machines and appliances associated with electricity. In rural American it might as well have been 1876…or 1776, because there was no 'revolution' down on the farm.

My future wife grew up in New Richmond, and she always had electricity. Her grandparents had emigrated from Poland, and spent their adult lives living and working in the Iron Range city of Virginia, Minnesota. For most of their adult lives they had central heating, in-door plumbing, and electricity. Since Mania's grandparents were the oldest people she knew, she just assumed everyone lived in a 'modern house'. She was totally amazed to find that the Moore's had finally gotten indoor plumbing only a few years before we had started dating in 1964.

But that was the dichotomy and the sense of disconnect in America at that time, and as an editorial comment, a pattern that I still see in many aspects of American thinking.

By 1928 there were two America's. There was urban America, surging with money and electrical power and all the benefits this new power could bring. Rural America was denied most of these revolutionary opportunities and changes because rural America was denied electricity. The big electric companies supplied electricity to urban areas where they had to string a minimum of lines, thus not spending a lot of money. Houses and factories were all packed close, so hooking them up was relatively inexpensive. So for every mile of electric line installed the company got hundreds of paying customers. You might argue the efficiency, but it was highly profitable for the giant electric companies.

These companies were not interested in supplying electricity to the rural areas. They saw no profit in stringing miles of electric lines to isolated farmers. The few farmers who were able to get electricity were charged from two to four times the rate of urban users. Just like every other major issue this battle for electricity entered the political arena. Rural people were Americans, they were voters, and they wanted what everyone else had.

Of course I am prejudiced.

I am a product of my past, and spent most of my life fighting against 'the big guys' in one area or another. I told you I have a prejudice, but then I am not running for president so I don't have to present a balanced report. And since I am not worried about being 'politically correct' I will tell you the 'facts' that I choose to relate.

So in my stories the early electric companies represent the Robber Barons that raped America in 'the olden days' and they are the sires of the dirty corporate bastards (both meanings of the word) I still rage against today. Rural voters eventually sought governmental help to find some way to get electricity to rural America.

The debates raged over whether government should nationalize electrical production, regulate rates, force companies to send lines into the rural areas, and what should this all cost.

Oh My God!

Communism.

Radical Socialism.

The end of Western Civilization.

The devil is winning over Christianity.

It was unfair for 'big government' to compete with poor little corporations. It was unconstitutional for government to get involved in the affairs of people and the states...remember that good old Tenth Amendment. Freedom and Democracy and Capitalism and everything 'real American's' stand for would be ground into the dirt by the heel of liberals with a social agenda.

Electric corporations argued they would be driven to financial ruin if they had to string mile after useless mile of line in open space just to reach one isolated farm. They would invest thousands of dollars to get pennies in return.

In some of the most convoluted arguments ever, electric corporations argued that it was ridiculous to supply electricity to people who had no electrical equipment! What would farmers do with it? And the not so subtle implication was that rural people were not smart enough to use electrical equipment. Just think of the old time caricature of the country hick that was so common not too long ago. There truly was a cultural lag between rural and urban America, but it was cultural not intellectual.

So what happened? That 'traitor to his class' Franklin D. Roosevelt managed to push the Rural Electrification Administrative Act of 1935 through Congress. The REA was created, and became more than a set of initials to rural America. The REA changed rural America in ways that we now just take for granted.

The REA created over 450 cooperatives (damn near pure communism!) that were made up of the people of a given area, and was managed by a board elected by the members of that cooperative. Now what's democratic about that! Can't you just feel American freedom slipping away every time you vote, elect your own leaders, and plot your own course of action?

The federal government loaned these cooperatives money. With this money the co-op could negotiate to buy large amounts of electricity from existing companies or try to generate their own. The co-op would string the high lines to rural areas, then set a fee for that electricity. The co-op literally came to your farm and made a plan for how many lines, outlets, and bulbs you could have. Like many farmers, the Moore's chose to have most of their share sent to the barn, and what was left for the house.

Now what happened when these country bumpkins got electricity? They went to town and bought things! One of the things many historians and economists, and anti-communists forget to point out is the economic impact of Depression era farmers buying electrical equipment.

Where do I start with the impact on the farm?

You have a windmill, so you hire a 'well man' to come in and put an electric pump in the well. Day or night, wind or not, you just throw a switch and water gets pumped out of the well. I think only rural people relate to a pressure tank. Electricity powered the pressure tank which would force water through pipes into the barn, and eventually into the house. Turn on a faucet, and water would come out! In-door plumbing became possible, but not before the barn was taken care of folks.

You want to send an old farmer to heaven on earth? Run electricity to the barn, and then buy an air compressor. Now you can have a mechanical milking system where Mr. Surge's invention would remove milk from your cows! Well fed water cups in front of the cow, electric milk machine under the cow, and the revolution had begun. In less time a farmer could milk more cows than ever. With the Holy Trinity of oats, hay, and corn a farmer could harvest more and feed his animals quality food year round, so the cows would produce more milk.

So now what do you do with the milk? When you only had a few cows producing a few gallons you put the milk can on the milk cart and wheeled it to the milk house. Again, the clever naming! The milk cans were put in the milk tank…don't get me started again…and the well was pumped. Ground temperature water cooled the milk, with the excess flowing outside into a large horse tank that watered the pigs. Ha, just checking to see if you were paying attention!

This milk house was made of field stone, and had a submerged dirt floor. In the winter blocks of ice would be cut out of near-by Yankee Pond and brought to the milk house by horse drawn sled. The blocks would be covered by saw dust, wood chips and straw, and this would be our ice house.

But now the problem was more milk than the milk tank could hold. Also 'big government' was violating people's constitutional rights by requiring that milk be inspected to prevent the selling of harmful milk. It is too disgusting to mention some of the things that were shipped before inspectors started to monitor milk quality. Let's just say I have known people who worked in a creamery, and to this day they will not drink milk.

The solution was of course electricity! We had to build a 'modern milk house' and attach it to the barn. The new milk house had to follow strict rules or the inspector could deny you the right to ship milk, and that would be the 'death penalty' for a dairy farmer. The building had to have a cement floor, and two separate doors that separated the milk house from the barn. There must be electric lights of a given wattage, but most importantly a cooling unit. I can still see it. It was a two door, stainless steel eight-can electric refrigerator that cooled water, then continually cycled that cool water over and around the milk cans until a thermometer indicated the inside temperature was at the proper level.

Oh the marvels of the age. That water was so cold. In haying time we would 'illegally' put a Mason jar of drinking water in for cooling, and chug it down after each load. It was so cold you got the instant 'ice cream' headache, but it was great and well worth the temporary pain.

To pass inspection that milk house had to be clean. There was a galvanized double sink wash tub that faced the south windows. But what made this a memory I will never forget was…get ready for the power and the glory…right there in the southeast corner of the room stood an electric hot water heater! The law required all the milking tools be washed in water of a certain temperature with a required soap solution. All equipment must be clean and free of any dirt or milk residue. When the washing was done, everything had to be rinsed. And then the tanks must be drained, and cleaned. Not a spot of left over soap or even soap film could be left in the wash tank.

Hot water! This was like Moses tapping the rock to get water, because like a miracle hot water just came out of a faucet when you just twisted a lever. Imagine water that came out hot, that you did not have to heat on a stove before you could use it!

My first 'real bath' was in this milk house! A bath before this consisted of taking off your clothes, sitting on the kitchen counter with your feet in the sink while Mom delivered kettles of hot water from the stove. While this was just standard for a little boy, my sister who was four years older than I thought this was a torture from hell. As she matured into a young lady of course this was oh so crude and embarrassing. And what if your 'town friends' ever guessed that this was how she bathed!

Hot and cold running water in the barn came first of course, or at least to our family. The evolution and revolution across rural America caused by the availability of electricity, probably went in different orders or different paces, but I am equally sure the impact was staggering.

Electricity allowed for the purchase of an electric refrigerator for the house. Like most rural people we butchered in the fall. What many forget is that the key reason for this choice of time was the ability to store perishable foods, especially meat products. The ice house might work for a while, but of course it would be useless many months of the year.

I can't speak for all rural America but for a while our solution was to have our animals butchered by Eggen's meat locker in Baldwin. Mr. Eggen would butcher the animal, and then charge us rent on freezer space in his businesses meat locker. When the family went to Baldwin to shop, they would bring home a weeks worth of frozen meat.

Just think of the subtle ramifications. Why did so many farmers raise chickens? Fresh eggs every morning! And just about anyone could kill, gut, dress, and cook a chicken in one day…and eat it all in the same day so nothing had to be stored. Chickens were near perfect; you didn't have to house them half the year (just leave the chicken shed door opened and 'they will come home to roost'. What we now call 'free range chickens' would feed themselves during half the year… there was always some grain spilled somewhere, and if you feed any grain to horses an amazing amount passes right through them. Chickens may pick but they are not picky.

Ya, Dad was crude and a constant tease. Before a meal Mom would fold her hands and say, "Let's say grace." Often before she could say "Bless us oh Lord…" , Dad would come up with something like, "Horseshit said the sparrow; let's eat!"

Chickens would keep many of the bugs and insects out of the garden and off the lawn, and even pluck at the grass. Your best meal also provided a built in lawn and garden service.

And another bit of Americana was that farmers always wore their shoes. I don't care what the condition or how many other clothes he wore, an old farmer always had his shoes on. In the winter of course the floors were freezing, and most farm boys grew up putting their shoes on before they put their pants on. In the summer a well trained farmer knew not to go out on the porch let alone into the yard without having shoes on. Chicken shit! Enough said.

A good farm wife was never sure what day let alone what hour the thrashing crew was going to arrive. Farm etiquette was the wife did not have to provide a meal if the crew arrived after noon. That time was considered 'set up' time and did not require a meal. So when the thrashing machine was hauled into your yard, the wife knew she had at least a half day to get ready, and most times she had over-night and the next morning to get ready. Now these old thrashers knew the rules, so they arrived at a 'great' cook's house in the afternoon which gave her more time to make a good meal, and over-night so she could make pies!

Something as simple as a quality refrigerator changed the lives of so many.

And how many refrigerators had a radio placed on top? That radio opened up the world for rural people. In 1923 KDKA out of Pittsburgh was the first radio station to 'broadcast' to the public. They sent out self-addressed stamped penny post cards (any memories there?) asking people if they had a radio, and could they hear KDKA. Of course this was all in an urban area. Now, because of the REA, rural families were buying radios just like their city friends had listened to for years. Before REA many rural men would drive into town to listen to the radio, they would get to hear baseball games or the Friday night fights. Men would go to town, often to a bar, and share some drinks and the radio with other farm men. But after 1935 more and more home radios gave the farmers their entertainment at home, and what breakfast would be complete without listening to the grain market, the stock report, and the death notices.

Farmers could find the weather report and coordinate harvesting. They could know the market, and predict a good time to sell those steers. Moms were no longer alone in the kitchen, they had the soaps to enliven their lives. Teens could listen to popular music and hear the vocabulary of the day and even get a hint as to what clothing was in style. The cultural gap between rural and urban was shrinking rapidly, only to be killed for good when television entered our world.

OK, back on my political soap box. The REA was so challenged and so hated by 'the powers that be' during the 1930's. Many ordinary citizens were truly worried by the apocalyptic fear mongering.   And what happened?

Yes, electrical co-ops revolutionized rural America, and thus all America. What else happened is that the co-ops…that means you and me, the rural American citizen… paid back every cent loaned out by the government. When you pay back a loan, with interest you have done a good thing.

And when you pay it back, and not default like so many true and honest and patriotic corporations have done, bitter sarcasm intended; well damn it, I think we and our REA co-ops were just behaving like what my vision of America should be about!

Once a month we would read the electric meter to find the kilowatts we used. Out would come the special REA record book, and that figure would be entered. Then last months small number would be subtracted from this months larger number to determine the amount used. Now go to the back of the record book and compare the number of kilowatts used with the price per kilowatt the cooperative had set, and that was your bill. Fill out the page twice, tear off the right hand side and mail it to the REA with your check. The left hand side was your on- going record.

This was one of my first 'real world math' assignments. Mom and Dad sat with me at the kitchen table and we did the math and paid our fair share to the co-op. We sat at the kitchen table with the Kelvinator refrigerator to the west, and the REA clock on the east wall. The REA clock told the time by using electricity. But it also had two little circles on the face of the clock. If the power was on, one of the circles showed white. But if the power went off, the red circle popped up. When the electricity was restored, you pulled the stem to white and reset the time.

But while it was red, the whole farm was in crisis. Modernity has its dangers, and one of those dangers was the almost complete reliance on the power of electricity. Rural or urban, when the power goes out the lights go off. But in rural areas when the power goes off, the well is dead. The electric pump can not pump water, nor can the electric pressure tank send it surging through the pipes. Now, you can not drink water, you can not wash, and you can not flush the toilet…something unknown to urban people because their water is forced into the house by the water tower.

On the farm, when the power goes off, the animals can not drink! When the power goes off the milk machine will not milk the cows, and the cooler will not cool the milk. If you were milking when the power went out that means the cows expected and needed to be milked. A milking cow's udder can crudely be compared to your bladder…if your bladder is full, try holding it until the power comes back on! So with the power off, we were back to milking by hand.

Many nights I remember Dad getting out of bed, taking the flashlight from the night stand, and going down to check the clock. Not for time but to be sure the power was on, and we were 'safe'. Remember now, we were rural. So when the power goes out nothing works. Pick up your fancy new phone on the wall. It is dead. So either by horse or by car, you drive until you see someone who had lights on. If it was late you had to pound on the door and ask if their lights worked. If not you drove on until you found someone who did have electricity, and hoped that they also had a phone!

Now you call your REA cooperative, which was located in Hammond, and informed them of an outage. They called a repair crew who had to drive around (often in the dark) until they located the problem. The problem had to be fixed whether it was light or dark, snowing, raining, or storming. All of this could take hours, and you prayed to God that if this had to happen it would not be at milking time.

What a wonderful yet tender trap this electricity has become in my life. Sure I tell war stories about my deprived youth. I am writing this story on my electric computer because my wife is using our other computer. I will soon print this remarkable epic on my electric printer because my wife is printing pictures of our grandsons on her electric printer. I have chosen not to turn on my personal television set because it distracts me while I type.

Soon it will be time for 'dinner' (it's noon) and I need to finish soon because Mania has turned off her kitchen TV and is running the microwave to cook frozen corn that was in our basement freezer because the side-by-side refrigerator-freezer is full. I absolutely need to finish now so I can check my e-mail, and then my cell phone for text messages, before I'm called for dinner. (It IS noon!)

Mania's cell phone is charging because she spent a long time talking to her sister in Seattle. I also need to close my window because I hear the air conditioner running. After dinner I will have to call New Richmond Utilities, because it seems our electric bill was high this month.

Chapter 8

**Where is Barry Fitzgerald
When You Really Need Him?**

I have obviously over-stated the fact that my ancestors were Irish, and Irish Catholic. But this fact is important in understanding us; and then you can probably pay it no mind at all.

Confused?

Good, because I see myself and most of my immediate ancestors as being contradictions. Because these contradictions both clarify and muddle an attempt to really understand my family specifically and maybe Irish Catholics in general.

To quote from that famous Irishman Sigmund O'Freud, (Yes he really said this about the Irish). "This is one race of people for whom psychoanalysis is of no use whatsoever." That Siggy! Now there was one funny guy!

As I said before, many people have asked me if I ate a lot of 'Irish food' when I was growing up. My answer was always, "No, we ate 'farm food'". Everyone knows that Irish eat potatoes, and the story of the 'potato famine' was the crisis that caused the Irish Diaspora. In the 1840's the Irish did eat more potatoes than any nation in

Europe, so the blight was a matter of life and death. But that is not my reason for writing. I am discussing my family, and my neighbors. And we all ate 'farm food'. My German neighbors, and my Polish neighbors, and my Norwegian neighbors all ate as many potatoes as we did. We all ate potatoes, lots of potatoes prepared lots of ways, and the only impressionable fact I remember is that some people were good cooks, and some were terrible cooks.

See, here is my personal take on the whole 'being Irish' thing. Hang on! There is a famous John Wayne movie where at the end of the movie it is revealed who really shot Liberty Valance. The shocked newspaper editor burns his data and says, "When the facts contradict the myth, print the myth."

I know there is the 'fact' of Irish history. But I also know there is the 'myth' of Irish history. And I think we are all more in love with the myth than the fact. At first it was a distorting of the facts by British leaders, then by 'true Americans' (this meant WASP's…White Anglo-Saxon Protestants) who had to deal with these 'immigrants'. But myths and propaganda work, and they work because there is always an element of truth involved. The early Irish WERE filthy; they did pack together in the worst of the urban slums; and they did fight, drink, and reproduce constantly. That's was poor people always did and the Irish immigrants were POOR! There is not one 'lasting stereotype' of any people that is not based on truth! But it is always part of the truth; selective truths that can create a 'straw man' who is a caricature of all the best or all the worst of that group.

I love the Irish, and the Irish Catholics, and am intensely proud of much of their history. But it was made clear by my family, and became obvious to my own eyes that the Irish were no better, and no worse than any of our other neighbors. I can not tell you much about the heritage and culture of others because I did not live their lives. I can TRY to explain a little of my culture, but be aware it is not a total coverage of my nationality nor of my religion. It is just about how it impacted me.

So are you lost and confused? Good. Now I will loop back and continue forward.

We did not 'eat Irish'. But we did eat good farm food. Mom was a good cook, but her recipe book only had about 3 pages. Whether for our little family, for special guests or for a horde of thrashers, Mom had those two basic guidelines. Quality and quantity. She had a limited menu, but what she made was always good. She did not experiment but relied on the tried and true.

Preparation took as long as it took! My memories of meals were that the food was always good, and there was always a great deal of conversation. It was not the 'topics' we covered because most of the talk was ordinary and mundane. I do remember a certain sense of democracy, because whoever was talking, the 'rule' was that three people would be listening. No matter your age or sex, your input was as important as anyone else's at the table. No matter the topic, people listened. Of course Dad would usually launch into some totally outlandish over the top teasing or sarcasm about what someone else had said. It was not evil sarcasm, but the kind that was totally funny, and made you laugh at yourself.

Dessert would end the eating. And we would then clean up and neaten-up the kitchen to finish the meal event.

So we did not eat Irish.

And we did not dress Irish.

The myth, wonderfully protracted by Hollywood would have you thinking we all dressed like a cross between a leprechaun and Barry Fitzgerald.

All the men wore 8-inch lace up work shoes, not green pointy-toed slippers. You could not find a derby hat or a tam in all of western Wisconsin, and a green vest or scissor-tailed coat was about as rare as a four-leafed clover. And speaking of green, who would have a green outfit, let alone any outfit that you wore for only one day, once a year? When your closet was a nail in the back of the door, your clothes were a little more practical. If a man had three shirts, at least two of them would be blue chambray.

And we really did not speak Irish. First of all, very few people 'speak the Irish' because that would accurately mean speaking Gaelic. Even by the time of the great famine, large numbers of people in Ireland could not speak their own native tongue. What we spoke was American Midwest English with an ethnic accent, and even the 'old brogue' was fading fast. The myth was we were all wandering (or the stereotyped staggering?) about like we had just walked off the set of "The Quiet Man"… " Mush-mush-mush- tural-i-addy"!

True, old Pat Kennedy could have been a clone for Barry Fitzgerald. And we did like to belt out "When Irish Eyes Are Smiling" at the end of some masses. In fact years later we sang that and "My Wild Irish Rose" at Mom's funeral at St. Pat's. And of course the 'final blessing' for many masses was the traditional Irish blessing, "May the road rise up to meet you…"

Ireland is supposed to be the land of poets and musicians. It is true that in ancient times a poet was paid like a king…he got the best cuts of meat...and I will return to this later.

The Irish did love music. But loving something and being good at it are two different things. If there was a gathering of more than three, Patsy always appeared with his fiddle. Have you ever heard cat's mating? When Patsy pulled bow across string angels in Heaven wept...and begged to be sent to join cousin Lucifer. Because of Patsy on fiddle or later Janice on the accordion many of us from Emerald had a phobia about music, and eventually a hearing loss that unfortunately came too late to save us from the pain of listening.

But notice that Janice was German, and she couldn't carry a note in a bucket either.

And how about the musical skills of our Polish friends just across Dry Run Creek? Give them an accordion, a harmonica, and a scrub board and they would dance 'til the dawn. Dance? I could 'dance' as well as some of those Poles but only if someone dropped an ice cube down my shirt and hit me in the balls with a broom handle.

And do the Irish drink? Sure, but so did the other ethnic groups. Go to a Polish dance and drink some of that clear liquid they use on dance nights...and the rest of the time they use it to remove paint, un-rust bolts, and run chainsaws...And if you danced well or poorly, who cared.

It wasn't until the radio came to Emerald that we could hear really good music. Arthur Godfrey would bring us Carmel Quinn and Jack Benny would bring Dennis Day. I am sure I am not the only one who thought of a white-washed thatched cottage, and even of 'going home' when I heard Carmel (we were on a first name basis) sing, "The Isle of Innisfree".

If I turned to an expert in language or linguistics or even a cultural anthropologist I might be able to phrase this properly. But I am going to wing this on my own. It is not speaking Gaelic that matters, nor even talking like you live in Dublin, nor even having the correct 'brogue' that matters. My personal theory about the fact, and the myth and the just plain reality of being Irish is the use of words.

The Irish love to talk.

They love to use words, lots of words. They love to hear themselves use these words, and they don't mind catching their breath while someone else uses some words. You can look it up anywhere, there are millions of 'Irish quotes', and most of them are so Irish. And that's my point…they are TOO Irish; they are exactly what an Irishman would say to sound Irish. These quotes and saying are so wonderful, yet they seem too practiced and too professional.

When someone Irish was talking too much, that means about normal, I would hear Dad and Irv say things like: "keep on rollin' wagon wheels"… "you tell 'em bloomers, you catch the breeze"… "and here I am without ink or paper"… and, "better crack a window, Irv's on a roll". Never say simply what can be exaggerated.

Most Irish that I grew up with were great people, but if you said to one of them, "Erin Go Bragh" I know most of the men would think it meant, "Some babe named Erin has 36DD's."

This is off the subject, but it fits. We were in church one Sunday and the reader was delivering the first and second readings. The second reading dealt with Moses and the Israelites wandering in the dessert. They had faith that they would be led to the Promised Land, so they followed the column of clouds by day and "...the burning brazier by night!" Unfortunately he said 'burning brassiere'. Now I suppose if 'Erin could go for her bra' certainly the Jews were allowed to follow a brassiere. But if you are following a burning brassiere, maybe it will take 40 years to find your way.

Have you ever tried not to laugh? Have you ever tried not to laugh in church? The worst part is that no one but my family heard it, or maybe we were the only ones listening, and so we were the only ones trying to hold back our laughter. If anyone had dropped a fart, I know I would have been excommunicated on the spot for my reaction. I knew God was already dialing and 'the call' would be coming. Squeeze your eyes shut, act like you are really praying, and think of something sad!

It is the love of, and use of words that I will admit just might make the Irish different. And here is where the fact and the myth intertwine. If I would ask Dad or Irv what time it was, they would stop… often lean on a fork…and say, "Now why would you be needin' to know that? You have no where to go, and your work's not done. And besides, if you would wait another two minutes I could tell you it was 10:00."

Now a good script writer could make this up. Picture old Barry Fitzgerald with his suit and vest, derby hat tilted at an angle, and a curved-stem pipe in the corner of his mouth. See, if you can channel old Barry and you would hear, "The time! Sure and he wants to be knowin' the time. The time! The time I tell you. And him standing on a load of hay in the middle of an open field with God's blue sky above, and the sun not even half spent. I worry about that boy!"

I can hear Dad turning his team and saying, "Now Duke, get your ass around behind you!" Over the years I have read about drivers saying 'gee' and 'haw' to their team, but I have never heard of anyone with Dad's expression. And of course it was typically over-stated and redundant if not stupid, because usually your ass IS behind you!

Now just when you figure every Irish sentence is going to be about the length of a Russian novel, the Irish have fun doing the opposite. Getting ready to hay one afternoon I asked Dad how many loads he planned on today.

"Nine".

Then he walked away. Nine? We had never put up nine loads in a two day period, let alone one. And of course I had fallen into his trap. The victim gets laughed at, and Dad gets to explain in great length just how many loads we might have. If we were going to push for a big day I would hear from Dad or Irv, "Might as well be a sheep as a lamb." It took me a while to figure this one out, but it is just a variation on an old idea. Go for it!

Like any child I made mistakes. I spilled at the table and I built poor hay loads, and millions of other mistakes. I never got a spanking; never a hand was laid on me. I do not ever remember being yelled at or being 'put down' in modern parlance. I have often mentioned being 'teased' by Irv and especially Dad, but it was never mean or belittling. I cite this because so often when I would screw up Dad would look at Mom or Irv and say, "We shoulda raised a pig. We'd be way ahead by now." I must have made plenty of mistakes, because after a while it was only, "…shoulda raised a pig."

Mom would ask Dad if he had gone to check on Mary and Irv. The answer was typical. "I only got part way in the door. Irv was throwing her on the bed. I think she's pregnant." See, Dad could have said "No." Or he could have told the truth, and said he had been there and they are fine.

But, he had to embellish (tell a lie).

Tell a totally outrageous lie.

Make Mom roll her eyes at him.

Make my sister and me giggle.

Entertain himself.

By the way, if Dad's story was true, Mary and Irv would have rivaled Abraham and Sarah as far as a late-in-life pregnancy.

I hope you are following my presentation. You don't have to buy it, but this is what I truly feel. We were not Irish Catholics of the myth. We were just ordinary people who carried an Irish trait for talking. See, we do have the Blarney Stone, and whether truth or fiction, we think we have the gift of gab. And when you are 'just talking' what comes out is not profane or offensive or insulting. It is just using the words God put in our heads.

True story. Well of course it is true; I am 'just talking'. We had an Irish priest at St. Patrick's who was delivering an impassioned sermon on the evils of bad language as the Commandment demanded. The priest was saying it was a sin if it was intentional, but he understood accidents because "…things can happen so God Damn fast on the farm…" Now this did make the parish smile, but what was really significant was that he had reached his audience. You could see parishioners looking at each other and nodding that yes indeed things did happen "God Damn fast on the farm".

OK, I have to top that with a story from later years. We had a dynamic priest who loved to spin great stories during his sermon. He even left the pulpit and walked the main isle as he re-told the Biblical story of Jesus being brought by his family to the Temple in Jerusalem. The priest told how Jesus left his parents to enter the Temple, and impress all of the leaders of Israel. And when Mary and Joseph and their extended family left to return home, each parent assumed Jesus was with the other or some relative. Actually this young twelve year old was amazing the leaders with his wisdom and knowledge.

In a panic Mary and Joseph realized Jesus was missing, and hurried back to find their lost son.

With great theatrical ability our priest had us hanging on every word concerning the worried parents and the wayward child. Our priest closed his sermon with, "And this was the first time in history that parents would say to a child, 'Jesus Christ, where were you?'"

There was a moment of stunned silence in St. Pat's, and then the whole building exploded in laughter.

I am not sure about the theological impact of that sermon, but a room full of Irish sure enjoyed the performance.

So much of what is 'talking Irish' is really a combination of love of talking, and the background of religion. To repeat my belief, I think every nation, every people have poets, musicians, and even famous talkers. Yes, I am prejudiced and have a limited background, but I truly believe it is the Irish that have a special combination of an almost 'melodic brogue', a love of using words, and seasoning of 'religion' in their speech.

Follow me.

Jo Ella was the mother of one of my best friends. She was a Norwegian from Iowa…an I-o-wegian if you please (that's eye..oh..wegian) and she taught me how to 'speak I-o-wegian'. You try being I-o-wegian as you are reading. Remember, focus on trying to be Norwegian, and repeat: "My name is Yohn Yohnson. I come from Visconsin. I verk in a lumber yard dere. Ya, sure you betcha." Well after about three practices I was about to order loot-a-fisk, and convert to Loot-rin. Oft-dah!

Now you try the same technique to be 'speakin' the Irish'. First pretend you are Barry Fitzgerald or Maureen O'Hara. Second, force you voice up to a slightly higher yet softer pitch. Now, smack you gums just a little, and say real fast, "Ah Faith and Begorrah." " Mush-mush-mush-tural-i-addy". You are about ready to order a wee sip at Red Higgins' Erin Corners bar!

So now you are almost 'speakin' the Irish' you have to have something to say. Well, no! My conclusion is you can just say words, some which make sense and some are just thrown in for ballast. "Well if I never see the back of my head…"

We hired a neighborhood 'carpenter' to come help build some barn doors. Now carpenter was always a debatable term in Emerald, because by the look of some buildings I felt God had banned the use of a level, square or tape measure in this township.

Ok, so we hired this carpenter named Ernie (which of course was Ernst) who was blind in one eye. Hey, you can't make this stuff up! If Ernie wanted me to get him a hammer, he would say, "Hammer!" Damn, that Germanic levity! Dad would want a hammer and say, "Now be a good lad and fetch your Father that hammer so I can be putting a nail in here." Well old Ernie would have the nail driven before Dad could finish his sentence.

Then either Dad or Irv would say, "Now look at that Ernie. The boy brought a hammer, and we be needin' a saw. Shoulda raised a pig!"

So now I have you understanding how to ladle on the words, let's pick out some of those words and expressions that are so Irish…fact and myth.

The Irish loved to talk, but they also were told they must pray. The Irish were very religious and very superstitious. So lurking behind every priest was a druid that would shape and re-shape your expressions, prayers, and even your religion.

So when a good Irishman was saying "Faith and Begorrah" he was really saying: my Faith (Roman Catholic if you please) and 'by God'. The 'ancient Irish' were superstitious and feared the wrath of God, gods, or 'spirits and fairies'. For safety sake, you covered all bases by honoring any and all. So as not to anger anyone, 'gor' was a made up name for God. Remember, "Thou shalt not take the name of the Lord in vain."

Not just the Irish would say, "God Bless you!" immediately after a sneeze because there was the real belief that the soul could literally be blown out of the body. An Irish wake lasted for days partly to make sure the person was really dead, and that the soul first got out of the body, but second so it didn't try to get back into the original body. In the first two hours of a 'wake' the windows were left open so the soul could leave; then the windows were closed to keep the soul out. People wore black to hide from this soul, and one reason for the typical Irish clay pipe was to make smoke to confuse the wandering soul. If you worried you could not cry enough, 'keeners' could be hired to come and cry for you. Plus the loud weeping would drive any unwanted spirits away.

I hope this all makes sense to you, because it does to me, and an understanding of history allows my 'language story' to continue. And to hopefully make sense!

Hang on, because more Moore contradictions are coming. For you see a Catholic could die, then they went to Heaven. But a superstitious Irishman was just never sure, so they hedged their bets. They didn't die; they 'passed on'; they 'went down the road'; they 'moved to a different room'; they 'went to see the relatives'. When Dad died Mom's sister Kate was there at the wake of course. She stood by Dad, and with both tears and smiles she gently slapped his face and said, "Now smart off to me!"

By now I know you are overwhelmed with the fact we prayed. And so did the German Catholics, the Italian Catholics, and, the Polish Catholics. Rumor had it that even the Lutherans prayed, but the jury was still out on whether they were allowed into Heaven.

So you would have the mass, and the mass was every Sunday and on every other special occasion like weddings, funerals or for a good harvest. If you got a proper Catholic calendar, usually donated by Cullen's Funeral Home, you would find every 'day of obligation' in red, with every 'opportunity' to celebrate the life, death, and miraculous event surrounding every saint, pope, and holy day by attending a week-day mass.

You went to mass. You said your rosary, by yourself some days and as a family on others. at wakes and during the 40 months (or so it seemed, actually 40 days) of Lent. You prayed before and after meals; you prayed before sleep and upon waking up; and you prayed in the evening if it was too dry or too wet or during a storm.

Remember, originally Lent meant fast and abstinence for the whole 40 days. The Vatican lifted these severe restrictions during Lent for one day. St. Patrick's Day!

So many Irish stayed Catholic, and Patrick was truly a Saint. In fact the behavior of most Irish on this day confirmed first by the British, then by American WASP attitudes toward ill-manner, immoral, drunken Irish Catholics. Even today, I don't think there is an 'ethnic based holiday' that rivals St. Patrick's Day. And to be honest, even today some of the behavior of Irish and "Irish wanna-be's" on this day are often less than flattering.

And yet the old superstitious Irish Catholic wasn't sure they were safe from the wrath of an angered deity. So what gets deeply woven into 'speaking the Irish' is prayer and 'little prayers'.

To an Irishman a prayer was a prayer; but so was a toast. Irish toasts are things of legend. Some would go on for line after line. But like I wrote ages and pages ago, many were just 'too Irish' and just too practiced.

It was the 'little prayers' that really impress me, because you see the little prayers became as much a part of accepted Irish fact and myth. And if I handle this 'properly' we can all learn some things, and laugh at the Irish Catholics of Larry's family. Please know that Mary Elizabeth, Sister Vincent, and all the priests of Erin taught us how, and encouraged us to 'ejaculate'. 'Ejaculate often', and 'ejaculate with intensity'!

Now that most of you are either laughing or highly offended, please also know that 'ejaculation' IS the correct and proper word for short, meaningful 'little prayers' that if practiced enough would become spontaneous and automatic.

It wasn't until later childhood that I learned from others that there were several 'non-Catholic' meanings to the word ejaculate. Ah...for the lessons taught not in class, but on the playgrounds. Red-faced we move on!

So the Irish were constantly ejac...ooops, praying. Before you could think you said, "Faith and Begorrah!" Now these 'little prayers' came in by the hundreds and over centuries, and some really were 'little prayers' but many are really just a manner of talking…Irish expressions. "Praise be." Now you could say that 'little prayer' so fast it might just be the period at the end of a sentence! Take a minute and think of the number of Christian sayings that start with, end with or are centered on those words "Praise be."

"Saints preserve" if you can't come up with several, but "Mother of Mercy" if you aren't trying!

If you were really stunned or wanted to end with emphasis you could blurt out "Jesus-Mary-and Joseph" but if you were only modestly moved it would be a simple "Glory be." You might get the hay in "God willing" but if you are not working hard, well "the deevil take ye…God forbid".

This slowly transitioned from pure prayer to half prayer/half expression to just plain Irish blarney. For example, a horse (or a young man) that got a mare (young girl) unexpectedly pregnant was a 'fence jumper' and the result was called a 'catch-colt'. If you were using a hammer and missed the nail, the resulting mark in the wood would be a 'rosebud'…and if you missed too often you could hear, "Are ya plantin' a garden Larry?" When asked how many kids the neighbor had, Dad said, "There are so many they sleep in pails."

See, we have totally left religion but we are talking in 'little expressions' that I think are typical of the Irish.

———

And then the 'expressions' can expand into full stories, and later shrink back down to simple but meaningful expressions again. Here is a story that I hope illustrates my point. Dad, Irv and I went to buy a horse. The horse dealer had a son who Mom would call "One of God's Special Gifts". Of course Dad made straight for this special child. Dad would as soon "be in hell with his back broke" than hurt a child, but he loved to tease them all. To Dad this child was as normal as anyone, so thus fair game for love! And fair game for that special loving, teasing of his.

Dad was the best horseman so he did a full 'exam' by checking eyes, teeth, feet, and back. Finally Dad pulled the horse's tail up and to the side. No big deal, but the horse had a polyp on the side of the anus. Dad pointed this out to the boy, and asked what that was. The boy looked at the horse; looked at Dad; looked back at the horse; then looked at Dad for a moment with puzzlement on his face. You could just see the boy trying to figure out how he could explain this to a very obviously dull adult. Finally he looked at Dad and said slowly, "That be the asshole!"

I thought Irv was going to pee in his bibs. Like in church I was trying not to laugh, and failing. But Dad was under control and having a man-to-man conversation with this very knowledgeable young horseman. I know this boy got very little 'fair treatment' but he was getting it from Dad. Fun, yes. Teasing, yes. But no 'put-downs' when you are 'just talking'.

So once we all calmed down Dad asked the little horseman if this was a boy horse or a girl horse because he was not sure. Very proudly and very naturally the boy shared his sense of nature and biology on a level that was so simple and yet so profound. He raised the mares' tail again, and pointed directly under the anus. Then looked at Dad and said, "See that? If it's down 'tween the legs, it's a boy. This is a girl."

We did not buy the horse, and The Three Stooges barely made it home we were laughing so hard. But another true story entered Moore lore. The story could be retold in great length or if a horse, calf, puppy or anything was born on the farm, all someone had to ask was, "Where is 'IT' located?"

It was 'the talking' that made the difference. Dad could 'talk' to anyone, and even carry on a conversation with someone about a topic he knew nothing about. His sister Elizabeth married a man who had an airplane and occasionally landed it in one of our hay fields. Clayton would carry on to Dad about his airplane, and Dad could talk right along, and he knew as much about flying as I do about Organic Chemistry.

He could talk to anyone, but I think he really preferred talking to children. He thought children were just like anyone else, so he would always get down on one knee so he could talk face to face. And he always 'just talked' to them. He never used 'baby talk' but they would carry on the longest, most animated conversations even if neither one knew exactly what the other one was saying.

So to be Irish maybe you have to have a little of the child left in ya! "God Bless."

Epilogue

I transitioned off the farm by going to college in 1965. I knew I was never going back to farming, but not because I hated farming or felt scarred by my experiences.

Dad and Irv had survived their 'life experiences' by keeping costs down and living an older lifestyle. Had I wanted to farm I don't think it would have been possible, because the farm had failed to transition into a modern farm.

Today when I visit with farmers I am so amazed at the transition. Farmers use computers for everything. Farmers now use GPS to accurately work the fields; we used to put an old shoe on a fence post and aim for that target.

I almost can't relate, but the operative word is 'almost' because I still can relate ... and I can actually 'feel' the transition, something that many 'modern' people simply do not understand. My sons had computers in grade school, my grandsons have always had computers .. .and Dad penciled hash marks on the barn wall for every load of hay we brought into the barn. Four vertical lines followed by a diagonal slash meant we had five loads in the mow.

Simple but effective!

But I am so lucky, because even now as I drive in the early summer, the smell of new cut alfalfa will seep into the car. Oh…the images and memories that come flooding back: the clack-clack -clack of the sickle mower; the whishing sound of the side-delivery rake; the subtle whoomp when the hay fork dropped its load in the mow ... and the half-second of air conditioning that drop caused. To steal from Simon and Garfunkel, it was the 'sound of silence'.

There was the smell of good leather (shoes, gloves, reins and harnesses) that were well oiled; the smell of new hay and old silage; and the smell of sweating horses. If you are hunched down on the metal seat of a John Deere side mower you are in a perfect position to enjoy many smells from a team, but I choose to remember two things; one is the special and unique smell of horse sweat; and secondly Dad telling me, "Now you know ... there are more horses asses in this world than there are horses!" And it made sense!

As I said before, Irv made his final transition on April 27, 1977.

Dad made his final transition on April 27, 1978.

And as ready as she was Mom's line must have been busy because she didn't get 'the call' until September 7, 1999.

But the land is still Moore land. And some day it will transition to Jeff and Mike. And then to Grandson's, Wesley and Ryan.

It is now down to 55 acres, but I hope it is Moore land until we either run out of stories ... or out of rocks!

Made in the USA
Lexington, KY
30 July 2013